Stina Bengtsson, Sofia Johansson
Navigating the News

De Gruyter Contemporary Social Sciences

—

Volume 46

Stina Bengtsson, Sofia Johansson

Navigating
the News

———

Young People, Digital Culture and Everyday Life

DE GRUYTER

ISBN (Paperback) 978-3-11-134028-9
ISBN (Hardcover) 978-3-11-134030-2
e-ISBN (PDF) 978-3-11-134065-4
e-ISBN (EPUB) 978-3-11-134071-5
ISSN 2747-5689
DOI https://doi.org/10.1515/9783111340654

Library of Congress Control Number: 2024942782

Bibliographic information published by the Deutsche Nationalbibliothek
The Deutsche Nationalbibliothek lists this publication in the Deutsche Nationalbibliografie;
detailed bibliographic data are available on the internet at http://dnb.dnb.de.

© 2024 with the authors, published by Walter de Gruyter GmbH, Berlin/Boston.
This book is published with open access at www.degruyter.com.

Cover image: gremlin / E+ / Getty Images

www.degruyter.com

Acknowledgements

We have worked on this book for several years, and there are many people who have helped us develop it. First of all, we want to thank the young people who openly shared their experiences of news and information in everyday life with us. We are also greatly indebted to our co-researchers, Signe Opermann and Natalia Roudakova, who were involved in the larger comparative research project, *What is News? News perceptions and practices among young adults in times of transition,* that the fieldwork conducted for this book is also a part of. Lynn Schofield Clark spent a sabbatical at our department and inspired us with her insights into theories, methods, research, and life in general. We would also like to thank our student assistants who helped us find research participants and aided in the transcriptions of interviews, in particular Paulina Åberg and Frida Tollesson who were part of the team for an extended period of time. Erik Björklund and Vian Tahir should also be mentioned here, as they spent a semester as interns in our research project, as part of their Master's programme in Media and Communication Studies at the University of Södertörn.

The research would not have been possible without financial support from The Foundation for Baltic and East European Studies, which generously funded the project that this book is a result of, as well as funding the ECREA pre-conference *Young People and News: Breaking Boundaries Across Europe,* to take place in Ljubljana in September 2024. The Centre for Baltic and East European Studies (CBEES) at our own university, likewise, generously funded our interlinked ICA pre-conference *Young People and News in a Digital World: Local and Global Perspectives,* organised together with Schofield Clark in Paris in May 2022, which gathered a large group of excellent and inspiring scholars on news and journalism from across the world. Our colleagues at the Department of Media and Communication Studies at Södertörn University, have, as always, been helpful, and have read, commented and criticised article drafts and parts of the book manuscript throughout the years of research, supporting our project from the initial idea to the finished book. A special thanks, too, go to the two anonymous reviewers of the book synopsis, who provided useful advice for the development of the manuscript.

During the work with this book and the preceding research project, we have presented the research individually and jointly on many occasions at conferences and seminars and have received useful feedback from other scholars in the field. In October 2021 we were invited to present our initial work at the Higher Seminar at the Department of Journalism at Södertörn University, and in May 2022 Bengtsson was invited as keynote speaker at the conference *Alternatives in Communica-*

tion Theory & Education, arranged by the ECREA temporary working group *Journalism and Communication Education* at Yasar University in Izmir. The Swedish school of Social Science at the University of Helsinki kindly invited Bengtsson to spend a longer period as visiting professor in 2021–2022 – financed by the research program ReNew – and to present our work in their Research Seminar Series in March 2022, and she has also been invited to present the emerging book at the University of Bergen in December 2023 and Linneaus University, in March 2023, while Johansson has been invited to present aspects of the finished book at the *Transforming Media and Communication Ecologies* at Jönköping University in April 2024.

Some of the findings and material in the book has been previously published or overlap with arguments that we have presented in academic journals. Some parts of Chapters 1 and 2 have been published in our joint article 'A phenomenology of news' (2021) and parts of Chapter 4 originates from the joint article 'The meaning of social media in everyday life' (2023), whereas Chapter 5 overlaps to a substantial extent with Bengtsson's article 'The relevance of digital news' (2023).

Bengtsson is the lead author of Chapters 2, 4, 5 and 6, while Johansson is the lead author of Chapters 3 and 7, with Chapters 1 and 8 jointly written. However, the book, as well as the research project preceding it, is a joint effort from start to finish, and we are both equally responsible for any error or mistake in the text.

We dedicate this book to own young people, Stina's daughters *Rut, Mina* and *Marta*, and Sofia's son and daughter *Rufus* and *Elsie*.

Contents

Chapter 1
What is news?

When Julia, a 22-year-old shop assistant living in Stockholm, wakes up in the morning, the first thing she does is to reach for her iPhone. Living alone in a small rental apartment, she spends the first few moments of the day checking her phone, still in bed, to see if anyone has tried to get in touch with her during the night, to then scroll through social media to get a glimpse of what her friends are up to and what is happening in the world. She is interested in fitness and training, and much of her social media feed is filled with videos and images of exercise routines, health advice and news related to a fit lifestyle, with occasional postings about politics or local events. She follows several influencers known for their expertise in fitness, both Swedish and international ones, and likes to watch their videos on YouTube to get in-depth insights, although watching longer videos is more of an evening activity for her. Julia's morning time with her mobile phone, instead, is about getting a quick overview of a range of topics that she finds interesting, setting her up for the rest of the day.

Julia's morning routine does not include much of what we would normally think of as *news:* the reading of a newspaper, getting a round-up of current affairs in a news app, watching the morning news on TV or catching up with the latest bulletins on radio. She is one of many young people across the world who might seem, at first glance, to have turned their backs on news and news journalism, or at least to be circumventing the standard pathways to access it. Indeed, the digital media context has made it easy to engage with news about political and social issues, but also to opt out of doing so (Boczkowski & Mitchelstein, 2013; Prior, 2007), and young people have for long been the subject of concerns about 'news avoidance', relating to worries that those who actively avoid news would miss out on important information about society, and therefore lose the ability to understand or be able to influence it (Edgerly, 2022; Elvestad et al., 2014; Ksiazek et al., 2010; Toff et al., 2023). At the same time, young people today increasingly access news on social media, where they encounter news journalism – alongside a wide range of other types of information about politics, culture and society – in a hybrid media context shaped by social networking, practices of self-representation, and the production and distribution of varied forms of user-generated content.

Is it possible to think of Julia's humdrum scrolling through such a mixed flow of content as a form of news consumption? It is arguable, certainly, that the altered context for news interlinks not only with novel uses of news, but also with more varied understandings of the concept itself.

This idea is prompted by well-documented changes in news production, including new practices of journalists, opportunities for media users to produce and share content, as well as changes in distribution, where the involvement of media intralopers (Vulpius, 2023), social media platforms and search engines has impacted the flow of advertising revenue, as well as leading to an algorithmically governed news dissemination. Today, a wide variety of online news sites, apps and social media compete for the attention of audiences, and platforms such as Facebook, Instagram and TikTok have turned into prominent news sites for audiences. As in the example, young people in particular show a decline in interest in traditional news formats (e. g., Collao, 2022; Galan et al., 2019; Papathanassopoulos et al., 2013), whereas micro-blogs, such as X (formerly Twitter) or Threads, can function as important sources of information for traditional media (Broersma & Graham, 2013) – but also as mass news media in themselves. Similarly, personalised news feeds on social media platforms, based on a mixture of personal posts, shared content, photos, films, videos, memes and adverts, can be defined within the sites as 'news', making rigid distinctions between 'news media' and 'social media' problematic.

News, for a long time considered a distinct commodity produced by journalists and established media organisations, is, subsequently, currently considered a concept 'in flux'. In the light of the transformations in audience behaviour, several scholars have started to question the way the very concept of news is used in news research, pointing out, for instance, that "all too often scholars rely on a traditional twentieth century notion of professional journalism to understand shifting audience conceptions of what news 'is'" (Peters, 2012, p. 699). Such a blurring of the conceptual boundaries of news is, arguably, important to study, as it potentially impacts not only how people access information about society, but also the wider role and function of news and journalism in society (e. g., Edgerly & Vraga, 2020a; Peters et al., 2022). A more nuanced understanding of what news *is*, from an audience perspective, is therefore crucial (see Bengtsson & Johansson, 2021; Swart et al., 2022).

In this book, we aim to further this discussion, based on a phenomenological study of young adults, aged 18 – 26, building on in-depth interviews and small focus groups with a varied sample of young men and women living in different parts of Sweden, conducted during a period between 2019 and 2021. Sweden is a pertinent case for the study of news in digital culture, as a highly digitised country, where almost everyone has access to broadband, and uses of smartphones and mobile internet are extensive. According to a recent international report, 84 % of the population access news online, including in social media, with social media, furthermore, used very widely and on a daily basis by almost all young people born in the 1990s and 2000s. Sweden ranks no. 4 in the World Press Freedom Index, and Swedes are more willing, compared with people in other countries, to pay for news, although only 33 % of the population do so, with lower figures among younger people. Together with other Nordic countries, international comparisons also show relatively high levels of trust in news, with particularly high levels of trust for public service media (Internetstiftelsen, 2023, p. 238; Newman et al., 2023, pp. 100–101).

We explore, in this specific geo-cultural context, how young women and men from different backgrounds perceive news, how it is integrated into their everyday practices and media use, and how they experience the role that news, as *they* define it, plays in their lives. Doing so, we follow a longstanding tradition of research that has aimed at understanding news as embedded in everyday life, searching for ordinary young adults' experiences of news as interlinked with mundane practices and settings, and acknowledging news as meaningful beyond its political function, while recognising everyday life as a formative site for communicative experiences and identities that may still interlink with the news audience as political beings (see Dahlgren, 2000, 2009). As will be discussed throughout this book, news and traditional news media may be seen, at least by *some* people, as a form of public 'good', perceptually linked to notions of informed citizenry and the requirements of democracy. For others, however, news, understood as something broader than just news journalism, is mainly experienced as something they need to navigate and manage their *own* lives, and they hence see news as interesting, important and worth paying attention to primarily in relation to how they think of the world they belong to and their own agency to act in that world. One area that the book provides insights into is thus what kind of information – from news journalism as well as information provided by other formats and sources – young people find important and interesting to pay attention to and stay updated on: in short, what kind of information they engage in and find worthwhile when navigating the essentials in their lives.

Navigating the news in everyday life

The book is called *Navigating the News*, which is in line with how we have approached news in our study. The idea of navigation provides a way of thinking about media practices in the cross-platform, or 'high choice', media landscape in relation to both news use and media use from a broader everyday life perspective. Brita Ytre-Arne, in *Media Use in Digital Everyday Life* (2023), uses navigation as a metaphor to describe how we use media "to orient ourselves as we move through our everyday lives", underlining the routinised dimensions of media use across, and in between, social domains, and the role of digital technologies in this: practically and specifically, but also socially and existentially (2023, pp. 8–9). Joëlle Swart et al. (2017c) use navigation to explore user practices in the contemporary media environment, as well as for understanding shifting user preferences underlying the evaluation of news. We similarly view *navigation* as a way to think about news use as a routinised, mundane, yet conscious and at the same time instinctive, way of choosing which media to engage with and pay attention to in one's media environment. Navigation, equally, implies an element of uncertainty and risk, and can be more or less difficult, depending on the situation. It requires a degree of skill as well as the right tools and knowledge, for not getting lost and for finding one's way – which, too, seems to capture the challenges facing contemporary media users continuously grappling with multiple choices and uncertainties in determining what information can be trusted and what is real. Everyday life in digital culture, then, is complex and multidimensional, not least as cross-platform environments multiply the arenas where people can be present and interact with others, and we hence constantly have to choose where to stay, when to leave and what to turn our attention to (Campo, 2015, p. 137). This is of course not something we can be constantly wary of, and those choices are neither consciously made, nor made in a vacuum, but often immediate, unconscious but built on our previous experiences, and socially structured. Navigating the world (of news), hence, includes the continuous acts of acknowledging and evaluating, following and drifting, interpreting and acting, as part of our routinely conducted everyday practices. *Navigare necesse est*, the old Latin quote says, and in contemporary digital media culture, navigating certainly is necessary.

Etymologically, to *navigate* means to direct the way a ship or an aircraft will travel, or to find a direction across an area of water or land. Today's media landscape, with its rich and diverse ecology of media technologies, platforms, content, formats and varied forms of distribution, has more in common with an open sea, vast and shifting in its character, than it has with how media, and news, were organised when primarily directed by large media houses in the age of print and electronic media. The shifting role of TikTok in the media landscape in Sweden during our fieldwork exemplifies this, as several of the young research participants, not without a certain portion of shame, talked to us about how they were drawn to TikTok and could get stuck in its stream of content for hours, yet perceived it as a childish medium, which they felt they should not be wasting their time on. Since then, the role of TikTok has changed, and it is today a more established platform, used by politicians and news producers as a way of reaching out to (primarily) young audiences. Hence, just as the sailor knows the sea, navigating the news is not conducted in a vacuum. As media users we walk through life with some idea of where we are heading; we follow the paths we have taken before, and those that others have threaded before us. And just as the ancient sailor kept a constant, yet disengaged, gaze at the stars, only paying them immediate attention when he found himself in the wrong direction, we often navigate our everyday lives in similar ways, somewhat intentional, yet routinised and, as such, without paying immediate attention to our choices or actions. To navigate, is, hence, an intentional way of acting, as it has a direction or a goal, although it is most often not deliberately or consciously conducted.

We have been informed by phenomenological theory and methodology when exploring how young Swedes navigate the news in everyday life. As will be developed further in Chapter 2, this means we have used an open approach, both regarding how we talked about news with the research participants (trying not to predefine the concept in the interview situations), how we strived to understand it as part of their everyday lives, and how we conducted our interviews, inviting narratives about a wide range of media practices and mediated experiences rather than a discrete focus on journalism or a particular news genre, as well as attempting to, as much as possible, comprehend accounts of news use in relation to individual 'life-worlds' and social contexts. And, just as the ancient sailors navigated by the stars and migrating birds navigate by the moon, we have paid particular attention to the equipment and platforms that contemporary audiences use when navigating the news in everyday life, here often their mobile phone and other digital media, as well as the social networks they provide access to.

Why news?

Before examining the perspectives of young people today, it is important to briefly consider the way in which news has been theorised as a particularly vital genre in media and communication studies, journalism studies and related areas of scholarship. On the one hand, the circulation of news has been linked to the development of modern democracy, and on the other hand, to the power to shape public opinion and construct interpretive frames and discourses on a range of topics. From Benedict Anderson's (1983/1991) influential notion of the newspaper as paving the way for an 'imagined community' of readers, holding disparate groups together in a common notion of belonging to a nation, to early critical analyses highlighting how news represents different social groups and constructs dominant discourses on social issues (Beharrell et al., 1976; Hall et al., 1978), news has largely been considered to *matter*, having significant consequences in people's lives and acting as a structuring and powerful agent in politics, culture and society. In the introductory chapter to her classic book, *Making News: A Study in the Construction of Reality* (1978), Gaye Tuchman illustrates this well in underlining how news can be "a window on the world", but also noting how the view from this window will change depending on the frame:

> News is a window on the world. Through its frame, Americans learn of themselves and others, of their own institutions, leaders and life-styles, and those of other nations and their peoples. The urbanized and urbanizing nation's replacement for the town crier ('Ten o'clock and Mrs. Smith had a baby daughter'), the news aims to tell us what we want to know, need to know, and should know.
>
> But, like any frame that delineates a world, the news frame may be considered problematic. The view through a window depends upon whether the window is large or small, has many panels or few, whether the glass is opaque or clear, whether the window faces a street or a backyard. The unfolding scene also depends upon where one stands, far or near, craning one's neck to the side, or gazing straight ahead, eyes parallel to the wall in which the window is encased. (Tuchman, 1978, p. 1)

News media, consequently, are often analysed as powerful institutions, which can enlighten the public as well as obscure their view (Curran & Seaton, 2018; Eldridge, 1993).

At the same time, news has been understood as a particular kind of product, drawing attention to economic, political, technological, social, cultural and organisational frameworks of its production (e.g., Deuze & Witschge, 2020; Gans, 1979; Hermida & Young, 2019; Schudson, 1978, 2003; Tuchman, 1978; Örnebring, 2016), while, at the same time, the idea about the crucial role of news in a democratic society explicitly or implicitly underlies much scholarly discussions of news. News journalism, in the latter sense, can be viewed as a 'public good', serving as a common ground for citizens and functioning as a basis for civic engagement and the construction of an informed citizenry (Clark & Marchi, 2017, pp. 59–62; Broersma & Peters, 2013). Key here are the ideals of balance and objectivity, which have a long history in the development of certain forms of news journalism (McNair, 2013; Schudson, 1978, 2001), but which have throughout history existed side by side with other journalistic norms, competing with more opinionated, sensationalist and entertainment-driven forms of journalism (Conboy, 2002; Johansson, 2020a, 2020b). Similarly, a strong, but not unproblematic, common normative ideal for journalism as a democratic force is that of independence and autonomy – from the state, the market and politicians, technology and other actors (see Örnebring & Karlsson, 2022) – with news journalism, likewise, distinguishable as a media genre aspiring to tell the truth, with accuracy an important ideal for many journalists.

The role of news in a democratic society is often linked to the notion of the public sphere, as developed by Jürgen Habermas in his 1962 thesis, translated to English as *The Structural Transformation of the Public Sphere* in 1989. The concept of the public sphere has been famously critiqued (e.g., Fraser, 1992; Negt & Kluge,

1972/1993) and redeveloped over the years (e.g., Butsch, 2008; Dahlgren & Sparks, 1991) – with one, for our purposes, particularly relevant rethinking provided by Couldry et al. (2007a, 2007b), who, based on a qualitative UK study, examined how civic knowledge and participation interweaves with various dimensions of media use. Couldry et al. emphasise how citizens' mediated connection, in reality, often is far from engaged, and neither particularly rational nor overtly political, arguing that the concept of 'public connection', as a description of a more fleeting engagement with news and information based on a wide range of different kinds of media, more accurately captures contemporary interlinkages between news, media, and civic knowledge and participation. Public connection, thus, points to the myriad ways in which people are directed towards a shared space for issues of public matters, where pre-political communication, entertainment and a range of everyday practices can feed into understandings of common concerns. Although such a notion can be problematised (see Hovden & Moe, 2017; Kaun, 2012), it directs attention towards the broader means in which news can function within the public sphere.

Another aspect to take into account is how digitisation has paved the way for novel understandings and roles of news in society, where the rise of social media platforms as key actors in news distribution and consumption, alongside the (uneasy) entanglement between these and news organisations, have led to a greater reliance on algorithms for news selection and the technological context for producing and accessing news (Bucher, 2018; DeVito, 2016; Thurman et al., 2019). José van Dijck, Thomas Poell and Martijn de Waal (2018) argue that this means that traditional news organisations, in a sense, lose control over news selection and the comprehensiveness of news, and that it places a greater emphasis on the individual in the selection and creation of a totality. The fact that news is often distributed via social media platforms contributes to a process of 'unbundling' and 'rebundling' of news content – where single articles or videos become separated from the original 'bundle', such as the newspaper, to be placed in the platform context. This also separates the previous 'bundle' of advertising and news product, as advertising revenues are increasingly shifted to search engines and social media platforms – which indicates a shift from news as a public value, a 'public good', to a personal value, as simply personal 'content' (cf. Broersma & Peters, 2013). Similarly, the emotion-driven dynamic of sharing on social media platforms impacts on what kind of news is produced and shared, placing the onus on user preferences, which, van Dijck et al. (2018, pp. 51–52) point out, contributes to how entertaining and emotionally charged content travels the fastest. So, although social media have been found to function as relatively important but contested spaces for learning about politics for young people (Bode, 2016; Holt et al., 2013; Shehata & Strömbäck, 2021), inspiring varied forms of political conversation (Highfield, 2016; Sveningsson, 2015), they equally provide a challenge to traditional news media. We have already mentioned scholarly concerns about 'news avoidance' in some social groups, whereas other current challenges include a more fragmented public sphere, with the risk of 'filter bubbles' (Pariser, 2011), incompatible views on reality and polarisation among different citizen groups (Möller, 2021), while the incorporation of AI services, tools and infrastructures in news organisations raises questions about journalistic autonomy (Simon, 2022). In relation to these contemporary debates and the increased engagement with news aggregators and platforms outside of conventional journalism, it is imperative to take an open approach to how young individuals conceptualise, use and make sense of news in contemporary digital culture.

Rethinking news

An important first step towards doing so, we argue, is to engage in a conceptual discussion of what news, in fact, is. A long-established definition of news defines it as a commodity produced and packaged within organised journalistic institutions – involving, among other things, an emphasis on newness, a truth-claim, a specific tone, and a set of particular values and actors determining what is newsworthy to an audience (e. g., Galtung & Ruge, 1965; Gans, 1979; Tuchman, 1978). With some variation, this is also the way the concept is commonly used in news research, even though it might be classified into sub-categories, such as, for instance, 'local' and 'national' or 'hard' and 'soft' news, or be distinguished by stylistic features, different types of media or content, or particular sub-genres (see Reinemann et al., 2012). Mark Deuze and Tamara Witschge (2020) have posited that journalism is transitioning from a coherent industry to a highly varied and diverse range of practices, which is a reason to look 'beyond' journalism and theorise it from the ground up, without being constrained by old preconceptions about its nature. From a similar standpoint, Chris Peters's (2012) call for scholars to look beyond professional journalism when addressing how audiences understand news (cf. Papacharissi, 2015; Zelizer et al., 2022) equally opens the way for more varied conceptualisations stemming from audience research.

Yet, although developments within the contemporary digital media landscape have contributed to a lively scholarly discussion regarding the current features and functions of news, it is possible to situate a rethinking within historical and comparative perspectives, too. John Maxwell Hamilton and Heidi J.S. Tworek (2017) argue that we must acknowledge not only the current changes in news consumption practices, but also the larger historical misconceptions in news and journalism research regarding what news, seen from a broader temporal and spatial angle, is and can be. They claim that the 'Anglo-American model' of journalism (that has dominated news research) is only one way of understanding news; one that easily gets challenged both by historic perspectives and current news consumption patterns, as well as by a global outlook. Disentangling the concept of news, they underline that "news is about more than journalism and existed before professional reporters and editors, before the idea of fairness and objectivity, before newspapers", emphasising how there have been "many ways of disseminating news throughout history", "from songs to jokes, to today's multi-platform media" (2017, p. 392; cf. Conboy, 2002). From such a broad sociocultural perspective of news, Maxwell Hamilton and Tworek conceptualise these transformations as 'epigenetic changes' that convert the essence of what journalism and news are, changes which are necessary to acknowledge when aiming for a nuanced understanding of what news can be today.

When thinking about news as a more malleable concept, it is important, too, to keep in mind how cultural differences can play into its meanings and functions. Elizabeth Bird (2010) makes this point in the edited volume *The Anthropology of News and Journalism*, arguing for a comparative cultural approach, which, similarly to what is suggested by Hamilton and Tworek (2017), would account for news outside of a Western or Anglo-American context. While comparison is not the focus of this book, it is nevertheless important to keep in mind how news can take different meanings in different cultures: a perspective that is also relevant for understanding news use in a digital and multi-platform media landscape, as global technologies are equally adapted in specific cultural settings. Such a reminder also points to the relevance of investigating audiences' perceptions and practices of news, where, in our study of young adults in a specific geo-cultural context, we have primarily drawn inspiration from scholarship examining news consumption from a qualitative, 'bottom up', perspective (see Madianou, 2013), relating to practices and meaning-making situated on a micro level.

Digital news in everyday life

Although an evasive term, 'everyday life' is used in many academic subjects to highlight the importance of habitual or mundane activities and settings that, while seemingly invisible and 'taken for granted' (Lefebvre, 1991, p. 24), condition a great deal of our human existence (Highmore, 2001; Bennett, 2005; Pink, 2012; Sheringham, 2006). Studies of everyday life, as both an intrinsic context for media use and as itself shaped by mediated communication, constitute an influential tradition in media and cultural studies (see Alasuutari, 1999; Bird, 2003 Markham, 2022; Storey, 2014), stressing the need for acknowledging situated practices and experiences in order to gain a fuller understanding of audience engagement

(e. g., Bakardjieva, 2005; Bengtsson, 2006; Dahlgren & Hill, 2022; Moores, 2000; Silverstone, 1994; Pink & Leder Mackley, 2013). As noted by Ytre-Arne (2023, p. 5), everyday life is, equally, the signal of an analytical position which prioritises human experience rather than technological systems, ordinary media users rather than professionals and institutions, and situated contexts rather than generalisable data.

We follow this tradition and its interests in the meaning-making, contexts and practices of news audiences, in routines, time and space (Bausinger, 1984; Madianou, 2013); social and family contexts (e. g., Hagen, 1992; Lull, 1990; Morley, 1980); social identity (Gauntlett & Hill, 1999); storytelling (Bird, 1992, 1997) and the way news plays a role in audience communities (Johansson, 2007; Wasserman, 2010) and to youth (Buckingham, 2000). Although there are early examples of qualitative studies of news audiences that have focused on dimensions of news consumption beyond informational and political uses, notably Bernard Berelson's (1949) landmark study, 'What "Missing the Newspaper" Means', this research orientation was for a long time less developed, relating to what Barbie Zelizer (2004) has highlighted as a tension between cultural studies and the study of journalism, with the former focusing on subjectivities and the construction of meaning, and the latter emphasising the categories of facts, truth and reality as objects of analysis. As argued by Bird (1997, 2000, 2011) though, news audiences often pay sporadic attention to news and make sense of it based on its narrative dimensions or in relation to social interaction and 'news talk' with other people, underlining the importance of situating our understanding of news use in its everyday context – but also of understanding this as part of *culture*. Writing from an anthropological perspective, Bird outlines what such a 'cultural approach' can entail:

> An anthropological (or cultural) approach to journalism sees news embedded in everyday practices. It may focus on the way real people – professional journalists or newsmakers in the broadest sense – are able to turn events into stories. (...) It may also explore how news circulates or is received, as stories take on new meanings in the telling. Or it may focus on news narratives and a discussion of what meanings come to dominate in particular settings. And perhaps more than other scholars of news, anthropologists are open to see news as a process that operates in forms outside of the traditional definitions of journalism.
>
> (Bird, 2010, p. 14)

Bird's suggestion appears to point forward towards the current surge in scholarly interest in news audiences, deemed an 'audience turn' in the study of news and journalism (see Costera Meijer, 2020; Swart et al., 2022).[1] Here, the shifting condi-

---

1 Although there are continuities between earlier qualitative news research, taking a 'cultural' approach, and that which has emerged more recently as part of the 'audience turn' in journalism

tions for producing, distributing and using news have sparked an interest in scholarly approaches to news in everyday life, emphasising, for instance, multi-platform news use and mobility as crucial elements in contemporary news experiences (Jansson & Lindell, 2015; Picone et al., 2015), and how emerging practices such as 'checking', 'sharing', 'clicking' and 'linking' (Costera Meijer & Groot Kormelink, 2015) become part of assembled 'news repertoires' increasingly integrated into other daily activities (e. g., Peters & Schrøder, 2018; Schrøder, 2015; Swart et al., 2016; Vulpius, 2023); blurring the earlier fixed times of news as well as traditional news geographies (Phillips, 2012). Another area concerns how digital contexts correlate with distinct forms of news use, including routine surveillance, incidental news exposure and directed consumption (Antunovic et al., 2018), as well as how the material and sensorial dimensions of digital news consumption impact on users' engagement with news content, situated in specific physical movements and mindsets (Groot Kormelink & Costera Meijer, 2019).

A particularly important strand of research, for us, has attempted to *reconceptualise* news in the light of such changes. Joëlle Swart, Chris Peters and Marcel Broersma (2017b) provide key theoretical rethinking of news in relation to public connection, whereas Cory L. Armstrong et al. (2015) challenge well-established ideas of news values based on audiences' own evaluations. Irene Costera Meijer and Tim Groot Kormelink's (2015) influential study of news consumption likewise reveals a broadening definition of what counts as news according to audiences: not only events described by journalists, but all types of content that are new, from developments in the personal life of one's Facebook friends, or opinions on Twitter, to information from specific websites of interest. Stephanie Edgerly and Emily Vraga (2020a, 2020b) similarly have suggested the term 'news-ness', defined as "the extent to which audiences characterize a specific piece of media as news" (2020b, p. 420), for capturing more varied responses to news on an audience level. Lynn Schofield Clark and Regina Marchi's (2017) extensive ethnographic study of teenage news use, furthermore, explores teenagers' news practices and mediated political engagement for an empirically grounded understanding of how news fits into their lives. They refer to 'connective journalism' when describing the news orientation of the youth, emphasising practices around sharing and participation in the making of a story as dimensions of political engagement, and exploring how young people evaluate news items and other kinds of information partly circumventing conventional news journalism.

---

studies, it seems that there are few links made within the latter to the former. It is our view that such links could strengthen current scholarship, by providing historical context and further addressing the cultural functions of news.

Two recent Scandinavian studies have also underlined new understandings of people's ways of accessing and understanding news journalism and other kinds of information. Peters et al. (2022) show how young Danes use a wide array of media content – beyond news journalism, and including blogs, podcasts and influencers – to stay informed about the world – whereas Henrik Örnebring and Erika Hellekant Rowe, in a study of hyperlocal information contexts that more or less equates 'news' and 'information', for example state that "for some people the local grocery store is probably more important than any traditional news outlet in terms of influencing how they act in their everyday, community lives and how they orient themselves towards the world" (2022, p. 40). In *Changing News Use, Unchanged News Experience*, finally, Irene Costera Meijer and Tim Groot Kormelink (2020) argue that even though the practices of using news have changed substantially from the mid-2000s to today, the experience of using news may not be as different as sometimes believed.

Such work opens up for continued enquiry into the category of news itself, while raising further questions about its meanings to audiences. Young adults can be seen as a group particularly affected by the developments characterised so far in this introduction, as young people are the most avid users of social media, and young adults represent a dynamic life stage shaped by the passage from youth to adulthood, where we develop an adult identity and encounter civic responsibilities, as well forming media practices likely to continue later in life (see Bolin, 2017). Young adults today also share the experience of growing up alongside the expansion of social media, as well as in environments where the consumption of news in public life has gradually become less visible, due to the shift towards personal and digital devices for news use (see Peters et al., 2022, p. 63, Peters & Schrøder, 2018). And while there for long has been an intense academic interest in studying young people's news use from a political or citizen point of view, in this book we pay attention to a range of situated news experiences and practices of a more mundane character. It will hence add insights into how news is perceived and engaged with by a broad variety of young adults, where some hold a deep societal engagement, but where the majority are, at an everyday level, mostly concerned with their own day-to-day life.

Navigating the book

This book builds on extensive fieldwork conducted in Sweden between 2019 and 2021. We have attempted to stay close to our empirical material and strived to include our participants' voices in the book as much as possible, to allow the readers to catch glimpses of the stories, expressions and dialogues of the research participants. This introductory chapter as well as the following chapter are mainly theoretical, whereas the remaining parts of the book provide a pendulum between examples and discussions of the empirical material in the light of specific theoretical concepts and ideas. The themes dealt with, in part, follow concepts that for long have been at the core of journalism studies, such as relevance, trust and news as narrative, where we use what the young adults found particularly interesting to talk about to guide us through the material. The chapters are also partly organised along the way that the interviews and focus groups were set up, where we started by asking for accounts of an ordinary 'media day', moving on to more specific or challenging subjects.

Having introduced the book and fields of research in this chapter, Chapter 2 presents the theoretical and methodological framework for analysis, introducing main theoretical concepts and analytical perspectives that have guided our research. It starts by outlining how a phenomenological approach can help researchers move beyond a focus on news solely as a source of information, underlining how attention to audiences' everyday practices and experiences of digital news can broaden the analytical approach. In this chapter, we underline 'bracketing' as an important concept that is both part of our theoretical framework and guides the research methods, as well as introducing the 'media day' as a specific approach to understanding news as part of everyday life.

Chapter 3 discusses how the young adults in our study describe how they come across and relate to news in relation to a wide range of media formats and content. Central to the chapter is the analysis of news encounters as interlinked with social media use, highlighting the blurring boundaries between news and social media from a young audience perspective. In the chapter, we argue that the notion of news can encompass more than merely the product of journalism, and include information gained from influencers, memes and social media personalities, but also emphasise how news and other types of information can appear, to a young audience, as part of an automated flow, with the notion of news as 'just appearing' underlined in the chapter.

Chapter 4 focuses on the everyday practices and interests relating to news use. It looks at three dimensions of news use in the young adults' everyday life, including spatiotemporal news practices and the meaning-making around these, as well as the areas that the young adults are interested in getting information about. It introduces how the participants constructed distinctions between 'big and small news', and the relation between news journalism as 'world news' and other news relating more immediately to their everyday life.

Chapter 5 presents an analysis of how the young adults understand how news, seen from a broader perspective, is relevant to them, and why. Based on an analysis of young people's notions of news relevance as understood through the phenomenological concept of the *structure of relevance*, the chapter details how news becomes meaningful in relation to different dimensions of the participants' lives, discussing what this perspective means for the understanding of news in digital culture.

In Chapter 6 ideas about facts, events and storytelling are discussed in relation to how these categories are viewed by young people when relating to digitised news. Departing particularly from theories about news and journalism by Gaye Tuchman and Walter Benjamin, as well as the phenomenological concept of *horizon*, the chapter examines the meaning-making processes around digitised news by young audiences as well as their views on news journalism versus other types of 'news'. It presents the argument that the digitisation of news has emphasised the role of facts in news, but in this has also made journalists and journalism less interesting from an everyday life perspective.

Chapter 7 focuses on the question of what young people trust in news, by examining how they talk about issues of trust and how they articulate what are deemed to be trustworthy sources of news and information, and why. The chapter makes a distinction between common *ideas* of trustworthy sources, including certain brands of legacy media, and *practices*, relating to the more frequent reliance on social media for obtaining news and information, and develops a discussion about how young audiences attempt to come to grips with this dilemma by relying on a range of micro-practices to evaluate different kinds of information.

Finally, Chapter 8 summarises and synthesises the conclusions of the varied analyses. Based on our analyses about news practices, meaning-making and spatio-temporal directedness in the understanding of 'news' among our young participants, we elaborate on the notion of *synchronisation*, and how digital, and particularly social, media have changed the temporal organisation of news today, and hence also the way in which it relates news users to the world around them. In line with this, the chapter further proposes that our contemporary digital culture has many similarities with how news was distributed, used and perceived before printed communication dominated the world.

Chapter 2
The 'media day': A phenomenological approach

As discussed in the introductory chapter, technological developments have changed the format, distribution and consumption of news, creating methodological challenges for researching news and calling for innovative ways of studying its audiences. In this chapter we discuss how it is possible to study news use if we have to leave behind agreed-upon understandings and definitions, to better understand young people's viewpoints. Such an endeavour, however, requires careful consideration of methodological obstacles and potential ways of overcoming these. How do we study something when its terminologies seem to be shifting? How is it possible to 'bracket' the way that news has been defined for decades, even centuries, in order to explore other potential outlooks for what it can be? To meet these challenges, we have developed a methodological approach to news in a state of 'flux' building on phenomenological theory. In this chapter we will develop this approach and describe the material and methods used for our empirical analysis.

Our aim with this book is to understand the perceptions and practices of news from an audience perspective, anchored in its mundane everyday contexts. Some scholars have recently argued for a 'radical user perspective' to come to terms with the contemporary struggles of capturing the meanings of news in a hybrid, multi-platform media landscape (Picone et al., 2015; Swart et al., 2022). Taking such a position, however, means that scholars have to be willing to study news as comprehended beyond news journalism, which, if taken seriously, poses an epistemological dilemma, where defining what news is today is part of the analytical process, which includes tackling the paradox that comes with leaving a prefixed definition of news.

In the chapter, we outline how some of the philosophical and theoretical thinking developed within phenomenology can be drawn on as an analytical resource for meeting this challenge, with phenomenology identified as a way to approach the world and the phenomena within it with 'wonder', creating "an openness to the world and a wondering attentiveness" (Van Manen, 2016, p. 36), which we have considered a useful starting point when exploring news from an audience point of view. Such a perspective means 'bracketing' our already learnt understanding of the world and the phenomena within it, and attempting to approach them in a new, clear way. In practice, this means leaving behind the preconceived notion of news as a commodity solely produced and packaged within organised journalistic institutions, including a fixed understanding of its core dimensions; newness, truth-claim, tone, values and specific actors determining what is newsworthy. The chapter describes, first, how the idea of a 'media day' can be used as a methodological entry point for doing so, to, secondly, discuss some of the key phenomenological concepts guiding the research for this book, including the notions of 'life-world' and 'Dasein', which, when applied to the empirical research, mean paying attention to temporal, spatial and sociocultural dimensions of news use, as well as to experiences of news as part of understandings of oneself and the surrounding world. Finally, in the last part of the chapter the design of the empirical study is explained and reflected upon.

Understanding the 'media day'

When attempting to get insights into ordinary and habitual media use, one means of doing so is to use the 'media day' approach. This is a methodological approach in qualitative audience studies, which we have used in several projects before this (see Bengtsson, 2006, 2007, 2012, 2018). It builds on the notion of the media as developed in the chapter 'The Media Day', by phenomenologist Henry Lefebvre, in his book *Rythmanalysis: Space, Time and Everyday Life* (1992/2013). Here he argues that "the media enter into the everyday: even more: they *contribute to producing it*" (Lefebvre 1992/2004, p. 48, our italics). Leaning also on John Dewey's influential notion that "*society exists in communication*" (Dewey 1916/1923, p. 5), this double constructivist perspective means that it is not possible to understand the everyday without understanding the media, but neither to understand media, including news, stripped from its everyday framework. The 'media day' approach therefore means understanding media as inherently integrated, interwoven and *co-producing* everyday life. The method has similarities with the 'day in the life' approach (Gillen et al., 2007), as it takes the ordinary day as a starting point for analysis, but there are also some essential differences, particularly that whereas 'day in the life' methodology uses the ordinary day as a context for understanding media (use), the 'media day' approach places media practices, media experiences and meaning-making around media at the centre of the analysis, and explores how it is integrated in, yet producing and produced by, everyday life. This means it, in relation to news use, would focus not only on how everyday life contributes to how news is perceived and experienced, but also how news use co-constructs the experience of everyday life, taking notice of the structure–actor dynamic (Giddens, 1984), or what Couldry and Hepp have discussed as a materialist approach to phenomenology (Couldry & Hepp, 2016).

A foundational standpoint in phenomenology is that the construction of reality is, fundamentally, based upon lived experience, with phenomenologists such as Alfred Schutz, Peter Berger and Thomas Luckmann (Berger & Luckmann, 1966; Schutz & Luckmann, 1973) underlining that our reality, including the materialities around us, is socially constructed and therefore perceived and experienced differently due to previous experiences, interests and how they have been introduced to us. In the broader field of media and communication studies, there is a rich tradition of scholars who have used such thinking to understand media as phenomena, for example Paddy Scannell's analyses of the phenomenology of television (1995, 1996, 2014; see also Nelson, 1986, 1990; Hutchinson, 2020) and Shaun Moores's studies of satellites (1988, 1993, 2011, 2012). But there are also those who have used phenomenology for audience approaches, to understand how *others* – media users – perceive and make sense of varied forms of media, such as the radio (Larsen, 2002), the emerging internet (Bakardjieva, 2005), the media in general as part of everyday life (Bengtsson, 2007) but also of news journalism (Groot Kormelink & Costera Meijer, 2019, Meijer & Kormelink, 2020). As already mentioned, in an attempt to update Berger and Luckmann's canonical work on the social construction of reality (1966), Couldry and Hepp (2016) likewise recently called for a 'materialist phenomenology' aiming to capture the materially structured experiences of living in a world increasingly saturated by media.

In a recent scholarly debate about the use of phenomenology for empirically understanding human experience, scholar in philosophy Dan Zahavi has, however, argued that it is not enough to "consider the first-person perspective of the agent/patient/client to make the approach in question phenomenological" (2019, p. 900). Seeking support in classic philosophers, Zahavi claims that even though phenomenologists may very well be interested in the phenomenality of experience, phenomenological studies should be about "returning to the things themselves", as originally formulated by Edmund Husserl (1900–1901/2001, p. 168), and that "seeking fine-grained descriptions of the qualitative character of different experiences" (Zahavi, 2019, p. 901) is not what phenomenology is about. At the same time, both the rich tradition of phenomenological media audience studies, and the profound transformations of the media landscape due to digitisation and datafication, require us to question Zahavi's claim. "Returning to the things themselves" is increasingly difficult in relation to contemporary media, as many genres, including news, are undergoing wide-ranging transformations and media use is increasingly individualised. In terms of news, technological developments, intensified during the last decades, have, first, transformed news as a 'thing': altering its temporality, mobility, format and mode of address, dimensions that are essential for how we experience news and construct meaning around it, and including a process of 'immaterialisation' similar to other media objects. An example is how newspapers have transformed from physical objects to 'immaterial' things, merged in the materiality of the mobile phone together with a range of other kinds of content, at the same time turning into a more ephemeral and liquid object that may reach its audiences de-contextualised and individually framed (Papacharissi, 2015). Secondly, following from the above, news use has become more individualised, to the extent that the *meaning* of news may largely differ between users: news today is, for example, provided and made meaningful in different media and in very different ways by a young girl and her grandmother. Thirdly, we also know from phenomenological theory that the world, and the phenomena in it, are experienced differently depending on when and where you live, where you are heading, and what experiences you carry with you, with previous news research having shown that news is not perceived and valued in the same way by people that come from different backgrounds, gender, and life-experiences and -expectancies (Banjac, 2022).

This means that it is relevant to attempt to see news through the eyes of others in order to grasp the full complexity of its meaning, which we can attempt to understand through a plethora of eyes (and other senses), against the backdrop of varied contexts and with a variety of experiences as frames for interpretation. In this we follow Max van Manen (2019), when referring to Langeveld (1972), who means that phenomenology must be understood as both a philosophy and a method, where method means "a style of thinking and an attitude of reflective attentiveness (...) to what it is that makes life intelligible and meaningful to us' (Van Manen, 2019, p. 911). We are, similarly, inspired by Van Manen's account that *wonder*, as a fundamental attunement in empirical research, is the most central disposition of phenomenology, when aiming at understanding the world (Van Manen, 2019, p. 914).

News in everyday life and life-world

When developing our methodological approach, based on the arguments outlined above, we have leant on 'bracketing' (or *epoché*) as a common tenet of phenomenological understanding, meaning that we aimed at putting brackets around the well known and taken for granted regarding what news is, in order to fully grasp how news is perceived and practised by young audiences today. Bracketing is part of what Husserl called "phenomenological reduction" (Husserl, 1931, pp. 44–49), which is when a philosopher brackets her natural belief of the world and her common-sense assumptions (Van Manen, 2016, p. 27). Bracketing is an epistemological approach to getting beyond the 'natural attitude' in the natural (realist) sciences, and to not simply take "our natural realist assumptions for granted" (Zahavi, 2019, p. 903). For qualitative research then, Zahavi means, its most important aspects are its criticism of scientism, its recognition of the *life-world*, its developing of an open-minded and non-biased attitude, as well as a careful analysis of human existence, understanding the subject as an embodied and socially and culturally embedded being-in-the-world (Zahavi & Martiny, 2019, p. 161; cf. Zahavi, 2019,

p. 905). Qualitative phenomenological research should hence be theoretically and epistemologically informed by core phenomenological concepts such as the life-world, intentionality, experience, horizon, and so on (Zahavi, 2019, p. 905).

The most essential concepts initially guiding our work have been *Dasein* and life-world. Martin Heidegger's notion of 'Dasein' (1996), or 'being in the world', is based on an understanding of human existence as *co-existent* with the surround-ing world and *intentional.* This means it is situated in the social and cultural situa-tion at hand, including its background, experiences, and material and cultural cir-cumstances. Dasein is neither fundamentally free, nor essentially determined by its context, but relates dialectically to the world and its own existence in it. Dasein is interlinked with life-world; the subjective world of an individual, as it is per-ceived through his or her senses. The life-world embraces the interconnected total-ity of worlds, or realities, that a human being relates to, and can thus be separated into several parallel, and subjectively constructed, realities. Examples of such real-ities are dreams, fantasies, scientific contemplation and everyday life. According to Berger and Luckmann (1966, p. 25) everyday life can only be experienced when a person is awake, which excludes for example dreams during sleep from what we understand as the everyday. Everyday life from a phenomenological perspective thus constitutes a symbolically significant category compared with other parts of the life-world, and works as a reference point for other dimensions of it, as every-day life, in contrast to other life-world categories, is socially constructed and hence may be shared with others (Berger & Luckmann, 1966, p. 23). This makes everyday life intersubjective, but also subjectively organised (my 'here' will, after all, always be your 'there'). Everyday life also differs from other dimensions of the life-world as it is *material* and thus constitutes an ontological reference point of a qualitative-ly different nature. We have aimed to embed the young adults' experiences and thoughts about news in these intersubjective, and material, conditions and dimen-sions of the life-world, although the Covid-19 pandemic brought along some unex-pected methodological difficulties, as will be discussed later in this chapter.

Despite this, everyday life should not be understood as static or fixed. Schutz meant that everyday life consists of several, succeeding, social situations. A situa-tion is a demarcated project with a special temporal, spatial and social organisa-tion. In each situation, such as when we come across a piece of news in social media, we decide what is relevant to us and thus sort out the sensory impressions and aspects of events that, in the moment, seem unimportant. This situated struc-ture of relevance can for example explain how memories can differ between two people who were in the same place and at the same time. The individual situation in combination with the subject's current life situation and individual history (i.e., it's autobiography) define what is experienced as relevant in different situations. This determines and delimits what we perceive as self-evident and fixed, or fluid and negotiable, and each situation must be understood from its own context-dependent horizon. An individual's *horizon*, Schutz means, is primarily dependent on his or her social and cultural history, the temporal and spatial dimensions of the situation and the project in which s/he is currently involved. This means, for example, that we perceive a trial, and the court room in which it takes place, differently depending on whether we are there as a journalist, reporting about the event for a local newspaper, if we are there as the accused, as the victim of a crime, or as a concerned citizen witnessing what we see as a deteriorating society. Understanding everyday life as projects hence means that both material and social aspects of reality are experienced differently depending on the project, as well as the socially and historically dependent, interpretive horizon from which it is viewed. Another important aspect of our construction of relevance is the overall structural conditions in everyday life that we have learned to regard as natural, such as legal and other 'laws' of social behaviour.

Based on phenomenological theory, we can thus conclude that everyday life surrounds us during our waking hours and is experienced as routine and concrete, while the experience of it is context-dependent and socially constructed. The above provides a theoretical understanding of everyday life which is crucial for our ability to interpret what news, from an everyday life perspective, is and means to young people. Therefore, this study leans on a definition of everyday life originating from phenomenologist Henri Lefebvre. He constructs his definition of everyday life in the mundane, as deriving from:

> what is humble and solid, what is taken for granted and that of which all the parts follow each other in such a regular, unvarying succession that those concerned have no call to question their sequence; thus it is undated and (apparently) insignificant; although it occupies and preoccupies it is practically untellable, and it is the ethics underlying routine and the aesthetics of familiar settings. At this point it encounters the modern.
>
> (Lefebvre, 1991, p. 24)

This definition of everyday life is multidimensional, yet distinguishes everyday life from what it is not. Lefebvre highlights everyday life as a flow of activities, limited and constructed in relation to its temporal and spatial context. This means that everyday life is not limited to certain special activities (e. g., leisure activities), or special times or places (e. g., evening time at home), but is a space we reside in, framing our experiences. This definition also emphasises the importance of the subjective experience of everyday life (everyday life as the invisible, self-evident, that which we do not reflect on) and thus offers a phenomenologically oriented view. It provides a temporally and spatially inclusive concept of everyday life, emphasising it as a flow and focusing on what is experienced as self-evident in existence. Everyday life is also considered a combination of materiality and symbolic dimensions, where both the spatiality and other boundaries of existence, as well as the ethics and aesthetics of it, are taken into account. This broad, but limited, perspective is a guide for this study, and the perceptions and practices of news in everyday life have been approached in this way.

As outlined above, phenomenology takes human existence as its vantage point and explores how human subjects exist and create meaning in their everyday lives in relation to basic categories such as time, space and sociocultural relevance. As mentioned, Heidegger's (1927/2010) theoretical notion of 'Dasein', 'being in the world', relies on on the understanding of human existence as coexistent with the surrounding world and intentional. This intentionality makes the being of humans temporal in its futurity, meaning it is directed to the projects and goals towards which it strives. News perceptions and practices are integrated in this intentionality, as news users use and value news depending on what they find relevant (cf. Pentina & Tarafdar, 2014). We also know, however, that digital media have started a process of *desynchronisation* (Lash & Urry, 1994; Kaun, 2017) of news, in *timeless time* (Castells, 2000). But news is not only temporally organised, and nor is humans' broader existence in the world. Maurice Merleau-Ponty (1962) enriched Heidegger's predominantly temporal phenomenology by arguing that our existence is also spatially relational, as a "form of perception" (p. 281 ff.) and approached the embodied dimensions of human existence. This led him to suggest that our notions of time and space should be understood in relation to our bodily consciousness, as part of human practice. We know that digital media have profoundly altered how humans experience space, both from a general perspective (cf. Scannell, 1996, 2014; Larsen, 2000; Bakardjieva, 2005; Pink, 2011; Moores, 2012; Bengtsson, 2006, 2007; Tudor, 2018, etc.) and in relation to news (cf. Peters, 2012; Van Damme et al., 2015). To understand how media users perceive news, we must therefore anchor our understanding in their temporal and spatial directedness, their intentionality, grounded in their everyday life practices and the specific cultural and material context of news consumption, obviously shifting both between and within individuals, cultures and media environments. As phenomenological research has sometimes been accused of lacking a critical perspective acknowledging the "many and often highly charged political, social and discursive forces that contribute to life in particular settings" (Desjarlais & Throop, 2011, p. 93), we aim at conducting a 'critical phenomenology' underscoring the "political and socioeconomic determinants of life and people's living conditions" (2018, p. 95), in line also with Couldry's and Hepp's (2016) call for a 'materialist phenomenology', adding to the phenomenological inside-perspective a critical sensitivity to the social and material conditions that shape it.

Our phenomenological perspective, further, brings attention to how the basic dimensions of the life-world coincide with the basic dimensions of not only news consumption, but also of news values; time, space and (sociocultural) relevance (Van Damme et al., 2015; see also Costera Meijer & Groot Kormelink, 2015; Dimmick et al., 2011). In relation to space, Peters (2012, p. 701) has argued that "space matters for how we experience journalism" and that "how we experience journalism shapes our social spaces" (see also Schrøder, 2015, p. 74), relevant not least for the increasingly mobile spatialities of digital news. Additionally, Emily Keightley and John Downey's (2018) analysis of the temporal dimensions of news consumption is worth highlighting, showing that the interplay between mediated and socially constructed time in news consumption demonstrates a natural embrace of the multiple temporalities in everyday experience, and that 'zones of intermediacy' in news consumption not only emphasise speed, but also the various constellations of time in which individuals connect with social, cultural, historical and technological temporalities. Peters and Schrøder have, finally, argued that the complex news consumption patterns following from the shifting media repertoires of digital cultures demand "a more dynamic starting point around how temporality is conceived" (2018, p. 1086). Such attempts to address the temporality and spatiality of digital news consumption, then, point towards their relevance in a phenomenological approach to news, underlining the importance of anchoring our understanding of media users' perceptions and practices of news in their temporal and spatial directedness, and its relevance in everyday practice.

News in the 'media day': A post-phenomenological approach

In this study, we have adhered to what Don Idhe calls a "post-phenomenological" approach (Idhe, 2003, also 1993) and Van Manen conceptualises as "practical life-world studies" (2016, p. 23), directing the phenomenological analysis towards practices and perception of others. One overarching challenge with this approach has been to use bracketing purposefully so that we not do predefine what news is through our project design, to let news in the interview situation remain broader than just news journalism, while also constructing it as specific enough to grasp a widened conceptualisation and experience of *news*, and not just end up with discussions about anything that young people find interesting to follow in the media.

While taking our departure from Dasein, or 'being in the world', we aimed at acknowledging the anchoring of the participants' news perceptions and practices in the world they inhabited, also affecting how young adults relate to news in digital culture. As mentioned earlier, we know that Dasein has an inherent intentionality; an agency to decide in what direction it wants to go. This relates to the individual's possibility, in today's multifaceted media landscape, to choose what media to pay attention to, what sources of information to turn to, which topics to engage in, and so on, according to the direction the subject is heading in, and their interests. We started all our interviews with broad and existential questions about where the young adults placed themselves in the world, where they dwell today, where they were coming from, what they dreamed about, and where they were heading. The answers to such questions obviously differ a lot according to general sociological variables such as gender, class and education, and relate to more than mere interest in news, as the questions aim at capturing one's hopes, wishes and ideas of what is meaningful in the world. With such a broad approach we have also aimed at exploring the respondents' life-world and how it relates to news; how our participants perceive the everyday world around them, its content and limitations, how it relates to their previous experiences and expectations – also aiming at understanding the *structure of relevance* that steers their intentionality.

After our introductory questions we focused on our respondents' digital media practices, starting out with the initial 'media day' question: "Can you tell me about your media use on an ordinary day?" This broad introduction was followed by relevant (but sometimes different) questions about specific practices and their importance and meaning to the young people, including how and where their media use took place; why they acted as they did (and what they thought about it); what content they chose to take part in and why, and the purposes it filled for them; how different media technologies were used for news consumption in comparison to each other; and how news was experienced and valued in relation to other media content, as well as its wider social and cultural meanings.

Being involved and engaged in news practices, and perceiving news in a digital media landscape is also part of our intentionality, and we know from previous research that users use and value news depending on what they find relevant (cf. Pentida & Tarafdar, 2014; Schrøder, 2019; Bengtsson, 2023). To understand how our participants perceived news, we therefore aimed at understanding their temporal and spatial directedness, and how they experienced the frames of news production and distribution, algorithmic curation of news and technological gatekeeping, that frame everyday news practices but also challenge intentionality and agency among news audiences in today's algorithmically organised culture.

We have found inspiration in previous media studies conducted from a phenomenological perspective, such as Maria Bakardjieva's ground-breaking *Internet Society* (2005), in which she studied internet adoption among ordinary Canadians, and Larsen's (2000) study of radio users in 1990s Denmark where he, for example, theorised the distinction between 'listening to' and 'hearing' the radio (see also, e.g., Pink, 2011; Moores, 2012; Kormelink & Costera Meijer, 2018; Costera Meijer, & Groot Kormelink, 2020)). These differences in intentionality among radio listeners reveal the meaning of the radio in audiences' everyday life, and more specifically how it is meaningful in users' transformation from the inner (home) to the outer world (public space) and how they orient themselves in time (see also Bengtsson, 2006; Bengtsson & Johansson, 2022). Building on their, and others', work, we have approached news perceptions and practices with a phenomenological toolbox and approached them as immersed in the temporal and spatial dimensions of everyday life, constructed by the structure of relevance (Schutz & Luckmann, 1973). Our study, however, differs fundamentally from the above-mentioned phenomenological studies in one way in particular – as we study a media genre 'in flux'. This meant that we could not simply ask the research participants about news, as this would have narrowed their imaginations of what the study was about, and hence led us away from what we wanted to grasp. Here, the design of the study with the initial questions around the 'media day' provided a way to be able to gain insights into media and news use without predefining what they should think of as news, a concern which also guided the interview design. We instead designed the study so that we would understand how news is practised and perceived, to, in the next step, nail down what news is and means from a phenomenological point of view.

As suggested by Zahavi (2019), we departed from some core concepts of phenomenology when designing our study. The most basic dimensions are *Dasein*, that we used as a vantage point for our approach to young media users' perceptions and practices of news, constructed through the temporal, spatial and sociocultural dimensions of it, in combination with the *life-world*. When analysing our empirical material, however, in line with our abductive epistemology and process of analysis, we introduced further theoretical perspectives meaningful for understanding the interview data. As it is important to look at, on the one hand, news *perceptions* (the audiences' ideas of what news is, what makes it meaningful) and, on the other hand, at news as part of everyday routines and *practices*, we have analysed how young audiences conceptualise news in relation to, for them, vital information (actively, as part of their intentionality), as well as the more routinised practices where news is part of an everyday flow that one can barely notice (cf. 'hear' in Steeg Larsen's analysis) or actively focus upon (cf. 'listen' in Steeg Larsen's analysis).

The phenomenological interview

According to Zahavi (2019, p. 906), conducting phenomenologically informed qualitative research is not merely a question of being open-minded and interested in first-person experience. Zahavi and Martiny (2019, p. 161) also claim phenomenology can not only make a difference in the handling, analysis and interpretation of available data, but also in how data are obtained in the first place, for instance through special interview techniques. This means that phenomenological research is also conducted in a certain manner.

We have conducted our interviews and small focus groups in the way suggested by Zahavi and Martiny, 2019), which means adopting an open-minded and emphatic attitude in order to establish basic trust with the interviewee, engaging in a continuous self-critical assessment of our own preconceptions and biases concerning what news is, as well as engaging pro-actively with the interviewees in order to elicit relevantly detailed descriptions. This means starting our interviews and focus groups with open and general questions, yet probing the participants to provide concrete and detailed descriptions of their practices, reflections, feelings and emotions concerning news in the 'media day'.

As pointed out by James Morley (2019, p. 165) phenomenological interviews aim, as much as is reasonable, to take a 'discovery approach' to interviewing and to seek out maximally rich descriptions. As already noted, 'bracketing' can in this way be seen as both a theoretical approach and a methodology. For us, this meant trying to bracket our preconceived understanding of what news is, and hence try not to force our respondents in any particular direction in the interviews and focus groups, where the latter were designed to provide open discussion among participants. We have hence tried to understand what news means to our young participants, without implying any predefined conception of news.

We introduced our project as being about how young adults use media and information in their everyday lives, which described the focus of the research project and aligned with the interview questions, yet allowed us to circumvent taken-for-granted assumptions about news, as we were careful to not steer their definitions and understandings of this. Therefore, we did not explicitly mention 'news' as a term initially in the interviews but circled around the concept in the themes guiding the interviews and focus groups. Towards the middle-end of these, if 'news' had not been brought up spontaneously (which it often had), we gently introduced the topic to the participants, relating it to what they had already told us about their information habits, media practices and interests. This is obviously not without its problems, as such a mode of conduct may encompass a risk of just ending up with empirical material that contains information about anything that young adults find interesting in digital (and analogue) media, yet it was a way to allow for an open approach to how they would talk about news and information.

In this sense we are in line with Amadeo Giorgi's suggestion that conducting a phenomenological interview (2006, pp. 71–73; 2009, pp. 128–137) means that the interviewer should refrain from steering the interviewee in the interview situation, but not with Barbro Giorgi (2006, p. 81), who suggests that the phenomenological interviewer should not ask any questions at all (see Zahavi and Martiny, 2019, pp. 155–162). In our interviews, we tried to be as open to the respondents' own experiences and constructions of reality and everyday life as possible, but we did use themes to guide the interviews towards our prime interest: the perceptions and practices of that which is news to young adults. We started our interviews asking about detailed descriptions of the young adults' ordinary 'media day', and circled around the participants' *experience of* news perceptions and practices, which meant what kind of media content the respondents routinely paid attention to, found important, would find it difficult to live without and miss out on, wanted to stay updated about, and what this meant to them, later moving the discussion towards other themes such as trust in different kinds of media and sources of information, and their ideas about traditional news journalism. By starting out with the young adults' media practices – detailed descriptions of what the participants 'did' with the media in everyday life – we asked them to further elaborate on why they turned to this or that digital platform in a specific situation, why they were interested in this or that content, or would click on this or that link. This way of asking the respondents to, in detail, specify and reflect on their routinised media habits is not only a way to gain deep knowledge about what they do and why, but also a way to try to gain understanding of the process of *navigating*, as described in the introductory chapter. There are of course limitations to what an interview can give in this respect, but the respondents often burst out at the end of the interviews: 'This was fun! I'd never thought about how I do things, and why!'

Important to note again is that we, in the interview situations, did not equate news with journalism, nor normatively constructed news journalism as more relevant than other kinds of media content, and although we did ask our participants about how they perceived and constructed practices around news journalism, we did this late in the interviews (when it had often become clear anyway). Instead, we aimed at a broad understanding of the participants' general media practices, what kind of content and areas of interests they valued and found vital to be updated and informed about, and if and how news journalism fitted into that picture. This somewhat reversed way of addressing news turned out to be successful as a way to broaden our understanding of why and how young adults think of, navigate, appreciate, turn to or away from, news in everyday life.

Participants and the research process

We conducted interviews with 67 18–26-year-olds in Sweden between June 2019 and January 2021, interviewing 20 individually and the rest (47) in 15 groups of 2–5 participants. The individual interviews provided more in-depth personal details and the small focus groups illustrated common discourses and the social interplay in the discussions around different platforms. The respondents were recruited with the aid of student assistants using varied methods, including advertising in social media groups (e.g., local groups for inhabitants in certain areas), specific targeting, "snowball sampling" (May, 2001, p. 132), with contacts of contacts acting as "gate-keepers" (see Kitzinger & Barbour, 1999, p. 9) facilitating access to a wide range of geographical locations and social settings, as well as providing acceptance of us as researchers. Thirty-eight of our respondents were female, and 29 were male, and the group interviews consisted of people familiar to each other, such as groups of friends or flatmates, as contexts in which people might normally discuss various aspects of the media.

The young adults lived in varied geographical areas across Sweden, from the north to the south, in larger and smaller cities – including Stockholm and Gothenburg as large metropolises, and a wide range of smaller and mid-sized urban environments – but were also recruited from villages and mere countryside. Some lived with their parents, others in dorms, some in their own apartments and some shared housing with friends or partners. The participants further comprised a broad mix in terms of class, occupation, social and ethnic background, livelihood, interests, and lifestyles, with 8 students at a gymnasium level, 21 at university or other post-gymnasium education, 6 being unemployed and the rest employed part- or full-time at the time of the interviews. A small minority were politically active, but the majority were not, some used (social) media as work arena, but the majority did not. All in all, the empirical material grasped a large variety of young Swedish adults' media practices and preferences but must not of course be seen as representative of the nation's youth as a whole. Most of our interviewees can be described primarily as media *consumers*, as most of them used the media mainly to follow individuals and organisations and for interpersonal communication with close friends and small groups, something which is also in line with national statistics of media use in this age group.[1]

As such, the sample is relatively heterogeneous, allowing insights into varied settings and avoiding a tendency in social research to over-represent university students as a demographic category. Yet, it should be noted that this diversity

---

1 https://svenskarnaochinternet.se/rapporter/svenskarna-och-internet-2023/english/.

and the relatively broad age range within the narrower group that young people make up could provide a challenge in analysing the results as, for example, TikTok or Instagram are likely to be approached differently by an 18-year-old and a 26-year-old. However, while we make no claims at generalising the findings to a specific population, we view our participants as speaking from a certain life stage, characterised by a degree of flexibility in terms of life choices and the organisation of everyday life. In the analysis, we have acknowledged the variety of uses, experiences and understandings of news across the sample, while being alert to details concerning participating individuals and groups.

Due to the Covid-19 pandemic during the time of the project, most of our interviews were conducted via video link on Zoom, although initially conducted in face-to-face situations. As young people in Sweden in general are heavily tech-savvy and used to communicating and socialising via digital media, this did not cause us as severe problems as we had feared. We soon realised that individual interviews worked almost as well as they would in a face-to-face situation (although we only got glimpses of the material and social environments inhabited by the participants as background of their Zoom room); however, the group interviews did not end up in the desired open discussions where the interviewer mainly works as a listener, adding some comments here and there to deepen certain aspects, but turned out as rounds where participants answered questions one by one, often in the order of the Zoom room (cf. Bolin et al., 2023). We used the time we gained from not being able to travel across the country to conduct the interviews on site as planned, to instead enlarge the number of individual and group interviews, as well as limiting the number of participants in the group interviews to a maximum of four, from the initially intended five or six. Despite the mishap of the Covid-19 pandemic and due to these changes, Zoom offered satisfactory conditions for the interviews, something also found by earlier research (cf. Archibald et al., 2019; Wahl-Jorgensen, 2021). The pandemic still obstructed our initial ambitions to include 'think aloud' methodology (but some interviewees took and sent us screenshots of their media content after the interviews), which is why the analysis leans heavily on the interviewees' verbal constructions of their media preferences and practices. Our methodological approach yet provided us with close and detailed descriptions of what, how and for what purposes our young participants used (a broad range of) media in their everyday lives. Our interviews lasted between 1–2 hours and were recorded and fully transcribed. Transcriptions were coded and discussed according to an abductive approach, highlighting the moving back and forth between theory and data which was adopted for the analysis, emphasising the openness of the researcher to the perspectives of the participants (Seale, 1999, pp. 91–105). In this process, new theoretical perspectives and concepts were introduced in the analyses, beyond those guiding the data-gathering process as discussed earlier. All names were pseudonymised and details removed so that none of the respondents can be identified. In order to further regard the ethical aspects of qualitative research and secure our participants' anonymity we have also chosen not to mention the specific geographical place where our participants live, but conceptualise the geographical areas in which they live in five categories: *metropolitan areas* (including the three larger cities in Sweden), *mid-size towns* (including a wide range of smaller and mid-sized towns in the southern and northern part of the country), *university towns* (including the cities mainly dominated by their larger universities), *smaller communities* and *countryside.*

Chapter 3
Encountering news in ambient media environments

When exploring how news becomes meaningful to young people in everyday contexts, one starting point is to consider how it is accessed and made sense of as part of their wider media use. As discussed in both previous chapters, we can assume that news consumption in a highly digitised and media-saturated context can be characterised as a relatively fluid and less easily delineated endeavour, compared with more distinct activities such as 'reading a newspaper' or 'watching the news on telly', and that this shift has a particular bearing on young people. Yet, when browsing social media, listening to podcasts, watching video-logs or finding out about the latest online gossip, they, clearly, come across a variety of information, of which some can be obtained from established news media whereas some will be gleaned from sources and formats that may, potentially, be considered to be news, while unrelated to news journalism. To understand how young adults view and engage with news, we therefore begin by looking at how it fits into a broader media context.

This chapter provides an introductory overview of how the young adults in our study come across news, and how they perceive different kinds of news and information that they encounter as part of their everyday involvement with a variety of different media formats and content. In the chapter, we discuss the ways in which news is accessed and incorporated into these daily media habits, paying particular attention to news use as interlinked with social media, and highlighting blurring boundaries between news and social media from a young audience perspective. How do the young adults encounter news, as they see it? What kinds of media formats and content do they understand as covered by the notion of news? And how do they experience novel forms of 'news' stemming from social media platforms, including hybrid categories such as influencers and memes, as part of their wider media use?

By paying attention to the media practices and experiences of young adults, the chapter provides some initial answers to these questions, to be developed more fully in subsequent chapters. It begins by outlining some recent research on how audiences find and relate to news in a digital media landscape, sketching some of the central themes of analysis within this field of study, including the concept of 'repertoire' and different ways of conceptualising changing news practices. Introducing the interviews and focus groups, the analysis is then divided into three parts, with the first part discussing the research participants' descriptions of their 'media day'. The second part charts what types of news – as defined by the young adults – they encounter in their everyday life, ranging from occasionally watching TV news in the family home to continuous updates within a personalised 'flow' of information in social media. The third part of the analysis focuses on dimensions of social media as platforms for news, further considering how these impact on the young adults' ideas of what news is, and highlighting how media genres 'native' to social media, including categories such as influencers and memes, can sometimes be experienced as important sources of 'news', with an equal standing to more official sources of information about society in the young adults' eyes.

News repertoires, 'news-ness' and new pathways to news

Paying attention to what is 'new' in current news use is a common starting point in research within the so-called 'audience turn' in studies of news and journalism (see Vulpius et al., 2023), as we have discussed in Chapter 1. The focus on novel and transformative dimensions of contemporary news use partly relates to technological shifts, paving the way for different forms of cross-platform (Schrøder, 2015; Swart et al., 2016) and mobile news use (see Jansson & Lindell, 2015; Picone et al., 2015), as well as to new routines and practices, including 'checking', 'sharing', 'clicking', 'linking' and 'scrolling' (Costera Meijer & Groot Kormelink, 2015, 2020; Kormelink & Costera Meijer, 2019), with the habit of 'snacking', as brief repeated news encounters, especially associated with accessing news via mobile phones (cf. Molyneux, 2017).

One way of identifying how news audiences find and evaluate news in digital contexts is the study of everyday 'repertoires', which can be used to understand how and why people find and combine a range of news sources, while potentially rejecting others (e. g., Edgerly et al., 2018; Peters et al., 2022; Peters & Schrøder, 2018; Schrøder, 2015; Swart et al., 2016; Vulpius et al., 2023). News or information repertoires relate to regular uses of a variety of media, which are not viewed as discrete choices but rather as relational and contextually based, including orientations towards, for instance, a range of platforms, brands or genres, or specific regions or modes of consumption. News repertoires, thus, are not envisioned as synonymous with individual selections, nor do they necessarily overlap with news appreciation (Swart et al., 2016, pp. 1352–1354).

The notion of repertoires directs attention to how contemporary news consumption is formed within broad communicative environments, highlighting how people 'meaningfully fulfil their needs for information and diversion' (Peters et al., 2022, p. 64). It may, however, provide less room for analysis of other meaning-making processes, such as everyday social interaction and construction of narratives around news (cf. Bird, 2010, p. 14; Clark & Marchi, 2017; Hill, 2007), while emphasising, in some sense, rational – if routinised and contextually located – forms of use. Social and mobile news consumption, however, has increasingly been associated with haphazard and unintentional news encounters (see Park & Kaye, 2020; Oeldorf-Hirsch & Srinivasan, 2022), and some scholars have emphasised how social media use interlinks with 'news will find me' perceptions among certain individuals, who feel that exposure to news happen irrespective of their choices or actions (De Zúñiga et al., 2017; De Zúñiga et al., 2020; Strauß et al., 2021). Based on a qualitative study of American college students, Dunja Antunovic et al. (2018) make the case for how 'incidental consumption', nevertheless, is to be seen as an expected part of young people's digital news consumption, identified as a key 'stage' in this, alongside 'routine surveillance' and 'directed consumption'. Such research mirrors other studies that have underlined how social media use, overall, is likely to interlink with unintended news consumption (Boczkowski et al. 2018; Fletcher & Nielsen, 2018), which can be seen as more common in the news experience of the young (Bergström & Jervelycke Belfrage, 2018).

The expansion of social media, clearly, warrants further consideration of their role in everyday news experiences, where different kinds of social media platforms, on a user level, are subject to distinct processes of meaning-making (Matassi & Boczkowski, 2023), but equally contribute to information 'abundance' (Boczkowski, 2021) that creates new challenges and opportunities for news audiences. As also noted in the introductory chapter, it can, likewise, be argued that the interconnected system of (social) media platforms (Van Dijck et al., 2018; cf. Van Dijck, 2013) impacts on news consumption far beyond multiplying the points of access; an argument developed by Clark and Marchi (2017) in their study of how teenagers partly circumvent established news organisations by using social media for accessing and creating their own news, with information-sharing and other communicative practices central. Their work correlates with theoretical analyses underlining how 'the new networked spaces of storytelling afforded via online platforms', apart from inviting communication and sharing, can be characterised as *hybrid*, in blurring boundaries between information, news and entertainment, and as *ambient* (Papacharissi, 2015, p. 29; cf. Hermida, 2010) – signalling a more fluid character that can be compared with the idea of 'news-ness' for capturing audience perspectives (Edgerly & Vraga, 2020a, 2020b), as discussed in the introductory chapter. Such analysis, no doubt, will serve as an important backdrop as we, in the following, move on to discuss the empirical study.

News as embedded in the media day

As explained in the previous chapter, we started our empirical work by posing a 'media day' question, asking the young adults to freely talk about how they would use media on an ordinary day, and from there proceeded to discussions about their uses of news and information. This initial question often yielded elaborate answers, detailing how different kinds of – primarily digital – media played a continual, often crucial, part of daily routines. As in the introductory example of this book, a common description was how they would start the day by checking social media on their smartphones, while still in bed, and from then on use a range of mainly digital media to accompany everyday activities in an ongoing manner.[1] Striking to us was the overall richness of their media use, in terms of the range of media formats and content engaged with but also how it was continuous and simultaneous, encompassing a great deal of the 'life-world', sometimes making it difficult for the participants to fully explain. A media day could include, for example, watching YouTube videos over breakfast, listening to music on Spotify in headphones while browsing social media or news apps on the bus on the way to school or work, continuing to check one's mobile throughout the day to keep connected to friends and public issues, playing a computer game or watching a TV series on a streaming site to relax back at home, listening to a podcast while cooking, watching a film or a series later in the evening – and ending the day by scrolling social media, in bed. Given that we did not observe their actual media practices, it is not possible for us to have a clear picture of how they, for instance, navigated on social media, although many were generous in attempting to provide relatively detailed accounts when asked about this.

These accounts, which may be seen as indicative of 'media life' (Deuze, 2012), or 'deep mediatisation' (Couldry & Hepp, 2016; Hepp, 2020), as characteristics of contemporary life, likewise provided a picture of daily media use at once highly individualised and social, in that it largely revolved around personal and individualised streams of information, with the smartphone a central technology, but

---

1 While most of the participants provided detailed accounts of their daily media involving different media, we should of course be aware that the accounts they gave us should not be regarded as complete, and that there may be aspects of their media use that they would not be comfortable telling researchers or other people about. Examples of media use that might be considered more private could be the use of pornography, which was not mentioned in any of the interviews or focus groups, online gambling, or the use of certain games or dating apps. The latter was discussed in one focus group, in relation to how a group of female friends would look at dating apps on their phones in a humorous way together, but in general, these types of media were not mentioned.

equally incorporated ongoing networking and communication on social media. As explained in Chapter 2, most of the young people who participated in the study did not describe themselves as particularly active in sharing and producing content (although a few did), yet it appeared common to sometimes communicate with others in smaller chat groups, on platforms such as Messenger, Snapchat and WhatsApp, which they found more enjoyable and experienced as less risky than the sharing in more public spaces. It was also obvious, particularly from the focus groups, that these chats could be the basis for 'offline' social interaction throughout the day, too. For example, in one group with male friends, who were interviewed on Zoom, the participants in fact kept using 'their' chat group during the discussion, occasionally joking and laughing with one another about the content in the chat. At the same time, the social dimension, as well as the overall media day, differed depending on the participants' living situation, which varied from living alone, to living with a partner, flatmates, or family or children. For those still living with their parents, watching regular TV together with a parent or other family members could, for example, be described as part of the media day, including watching morning or evening news programmes together. In these instances, the young adults had not themselves chosen what to watch but appreciated the opportunity to connect to their families and to be able to comment on various news items together.

As would be expected given the participants' age and geo-cultural location, social media played a critical part in their daily media use. Using one's smartphone to scroll through and briefly 'check' a range of social media platforms throughout the day was described as a recurring habit, providing opportunities to keep up to date with friends and the extended social network as well as keeping abreast with what was going on in society and the world beyond the immediate surroundings. Samuel, a 23-year-old personal assistant who lived by himself in a university town, explained how his day was initiated in this way, with social media accompanying other activities, too:

> Samuel: When I wake up I check the phone for a bit, and then there might have dropped in some memes in group chats, or whatever. I usually start with some scrolling, for example both Instagram and Facebook, I check all messages and might write something myself. Then it just continues, so I sit down in front of the computer (...). A lot of TV and streaming. I rarely post on social media. I've just downloaded that bloody app, TikTok, too, which the lads recommended, and yesterday I was in the bath for two and a half hours, just scrolling through TikTok.
>
> (Samuel, 23, personal assistant, university town)

As emphasised by Samuel, the checking and scrolling of social media platforms could thus frame and punctuate the day, although it was far from always described as an active choice. This more habitual, or even compulsive, aspect was also exemplified by Ingrid and Tilda, two 22-year-olds living in a mid-size town in central Sweden, working at a school and in a shop, when discussing their motivation for repeatedly checking Instagram, Twitter and Snapchat throughout their day:

> Ingrid: As soon as you're waiting for the bus or go somewhere you check Instagram, and Twitter, and Snapchat, all the time. Because that's where we talk, or whatever. (...)
>
> Tilda: I completely agree! You do it because you're bored and have nothing else to do.
>
> (Focus group, 22, mid-size town)

It can be noted, thus, that the young adults' uses of social media were partly experienced as something distinct from active social networking or a determined search for news or other information. The continual scrolling and 'checking' correspond to the cyclical and brief 'scanning' that has been observed for contemporary news consumption (Costera Meijer & Groot Kormelink, 2015, 2020; Groot Kormelink & Costera Meijer, 2019), but when thinking about how encounters with news may interweave with young adults' everyday uses of social media, it is clearly necessary to acknowledge its routinised and more unaware dimensions.

In line with national statistics at the time,[2] the most frequently used social media platforms were Facebook, Instagram and Snapchat, which almost all the respondents used every day, followed by Youtube, Twitter (currently X) and TikTok, which many used regularly. Some discussed less commonly used platforms, such as WhatsApp, Reddit, Pinterest and Twitch. Although the participants' social media habits, then, appeared to follow user patterns for the specific age group in Sweden, they equally mirrored international research on young adults' social media use, in that different platforms appeared to play distinct roles in their lives (see Boczkowski et al., 2018). For instance, while Facebook was often described as a more 'official' platform, used, for example, for taking part in interest groups and finding information about work opportunities and social events, Instagram was seen as suited for following lifestyle trends, influencers and information about what was happening in society, whereas Snapchat appeared particularly valued for communicating with and keeping up to date with friends. Similarly, YouTube was often described as a platform that could help deepen knowledge about specific subjects or interests, with Twitter as offering interesting opinions, and TikTok generally described as a source of light-hearted entertainment at the time of the interviews. Such nuances, which will be developed further in the next chapter, are important to recognise as they necessitate a holistic perspective to understand how social media interplay in the lives of young people, as well as providing a backdrop to

---

2 https://svenskarnaochinternet.se/rapporter/svenskarna-och-internet-2020/sociala-medier/?gclid=EAIaIQobChMItPL-weW-7wIVQaOyCh0gdAEQEAAYASABEgI7R_D_BwE.

the enquiry into how news was encountered within the participants' overall media use.

News was not commonly mentioned in the first response to our question about the media day, perhaps reflecting how conventional news is not always prioritised by people in this age group (see Peters et al., 2022, pp. 65–66), and serving as a reminder of how news journalism, when approached as part of a *totality* of different media, is not necessarily considered a particularly prominent feature by young people. As will be discussed below, there were several participants who said that they would read an online newspaper or check a news aggregator app on a, more or less, daily basis, and some of the 'older' participants in this sample mentioned 'quality' morning papers, read online, in their immediate descriptions of their regular media habits, as well as radio news, whereas others explained straight away that they had a strong interest in news. Yet, these immediate connections to news were not common, and, in the initial phase of the discussions, news did generally not appear as a key feature within their daily media use.

There was, however, a widespread notion among most of the young adults of news as being *important* – a media genre of value to society (c.f. Casero Ripollés, 2012). Yet, when describing their own media consumption practices, it appeared less prominent, at least initially in the discussions. This slight discrepancy, which can be seen as something of a paradox also found in previous studies of young news audiences (Costera Meijer, 2007), is exemplified in the following explanation by Michelle, an unemployed 19-year-old living in the countryside, who emphasised how she felt it was imperative to follow news media, such as the popular tabloid *Aftonbladet*, at the same time as recognising that this was something that she aspired to, rather than actively practised in her daily life:

> Michelle: I think it's important that both myself and others follow the news media, like *Aftonbladet* or something, so you have an idea of what's happening in the world. I definitely feel like I should get better at that, because it's so important to keep updated. So that feels important to me.
>
> (Michelle, 19, unemployed, countryside)

Keeping up to date with the news, then, was regarded as an ideal and something to strive for, but on an everyday level it was not always prioritised among the range of available media content. This mirrored a previous Swedish study of how youth view social media as sources of public affairs news, which in a similar way found a strong belief in the value of taking part in news journalism and feelings of shame for privately preferring to instead follow more 'frivolous' social media content (Sveningsson, 2015).

Finding news

However, despite the tension between the perception of engaged news consumption as an ideal, and the actual day-to-day routines adhered to, as our interviews progressed it became clear that both news journalism and other kinds of information that the participants regarded as 'news' were still in different ways present within their overall media habits. As mentioned, TV news programmes were regularly watched by some of the participants, who explained how morning or evening newscasts from the public service broadcaster (SVT) or from TV4, a popular commercial TV channel, formed part of their routines. Here, *Nyhetsmorgon*, a morning news show on TV4 mixing 'serious' and more light-hearted news, seemed especially appreciated for being entertaining as well as informative. Likewise, some read free local newspapers every now and again, and many claimed to at least occasionally read an online newspaper, with *Aftonbladet*'s free app mentioned as a source of news in many of the discussions, alongside the SVT news app, and Omni, a free Swedish news aggregator app that was particularly appreciated for allowing brief round-ups of the main news headlines; a type of quick overview that many, in fact, seemed to prefer when accessing news journalism online. Furthermore, possibly reflecting how news consumption is intimately linked with social class (see Lindell, 2018; Lindell & Mikkelsen Båge, 2023), some of the participants from a middle-class background, whose parents had gone to university or who were themselves university students, also mentioned the two 'quality' Swedish newspapers *Dagens Nyheter* and *Svenska Dagbladet* as key to their regular news consumption. Others, however, regarded these types of news sources as inaccessible, possibly because of the more demanding content but also due to the price required to get behind the paywall for content. As exemplified by a 23-year-old shop assistant from a metropolitan area, the price of news could, in fact, be a key concern when choosing a news source, and reading a newspaper online was not necessarily something considered worth paying for:

> Tuva: The ones [news sources] that I'm mostly drawn to are the evening tabloids *Expressen* or *Aftonbladet*. A lot of young people my age have these apps, but mainly for pleasure and shock value than for actual news. If something interesting turns up I'll check it there. Often it's for free as well – much more often than in *Svenska Dagbladet* and *Dagens Nyheter*, which you have to pay for.
>
> (Tuva, 23, shop assistant, metropolitan area)

When the participants elaborated on which types of news journalism they were interested in and would meet in their everyday life, then, the emphasis, as in this example, was often on news sources that were entertaining or provided a quick, easily accessible overview, but also were available for free. The latter can be compared to Danish research showing how young audiences may view news as a 'free' resource (Kammer et al., 2015) but is also a reminder of how the price of news journalism can be important for some parts of the audience.

Thus, many of the young adults would at least in some capacity actively turn to different forms of news journalism, including the news apps that some had downloaded on their phones. News journalism could also be accessed as embedded in their social media feeds, where they, likewise, regularly encountered a range of other types of information about society from a variety of other sources, including influencers, video-logs on YouTube, Instagram Stories, memes, social media postings of friends and family, and websites from organisations and government agencies. It, likewise, became clear that for many, this kind of wider information but also some news journalism encountered in social media could be of a transnational character, with several participants for example being aware of and spontaneously mentioning some main English-language news sites, including the *Daily Mail*, the *Sun*, *Fox News* and *CNN*. In some of the interviews and focus groups there were also accounts of what Antunovic et al. (2018) call 'directed consumption', exemplified by how the participants explained they would turn to and actively seek out information from established news sources when a major event or something out of the ordinary appeared, for example in relation to Covid-19.

However, the discussions also provided insights into less actively sought after encounters with news. This type of news use appeared hard to pin-point, yet it was often mentioned when participants were asked about where they would find news and information about society – a question that some would struggle to answer or explain, or answer with statements such as "I don't know, it just comes to me!" Where news 'comes from', then, could be a difficult question to answer, with news as 'just appearing' a notable aspect of the young adults' experiences. As in the example below, when a university student in the natural sciences described her overall news routines, it could, for instance, be related to automatic 'push notifications' not always easy to identify:

> Beatrice: Well, I think I get these ... what do you call them, push notifications, from *Dagens Nyheter?* I think? I'm not sure, I need to check. *Dagens Nyheter,* SVT, TV4-play. I think those are what I get – yes, those I get push notifications from, so then I can kind of see the headlines. (...) But I don't think I read very much. In the morning, I scroll through social media for a little while, like Facebook and Instagram. And then I do check the SVT app. And I think those are the only things that I actively go to.
>
> (Beatrice, 25, university student, metropolitan area)

Similarly, the experience of news as 'just appearing' could relate to an algorithmic selection of news and information based on earlier searches and personal interests, as explained by Wilhelm, a 20-year-old IT technician:

Interviewer: What type of news are you interested in, Wilhelm?

Wilhelm: Well, it could be everything from some gossip about … for example, Johnny Depp, you hear a lot about him now. Or about Covid being on the increase, and how we're not prepared for the next wave, for example. Or it could be about a game, that there's a new release coming up later. So everything from entertainment to serious news, really.

Interviewer: We talked about gaming before, is it from YouTube you get information there, or?

Wilhelm: It depends, it can vary from YouTube to Google. If you open up your news feed on your mobile phone, you get a lot of news there. It comes from the searches you've done on YouTube and Google, which I guess depends on what you've been searching for, what they decide to show you.

Interviewer: So you mean that you don't consciously go in and look for that type of news…?

Wilhelm: No, exactly.

(Wilhelm, 20, IT technician, countryside)

The experiences described by Beatrice and Wilhelm are, arguably, not possible to fully capture using the notion of news repertoires, as these require some sort of active selection of platforms and sources, whereas the accounts of Beatrice and Wilhelm concern automated encounters with news that seemed difficult for the participants themselves to pin-point or identify. Instead, these kinds of descriptions draw attention to how exposure to news can appear as part of an ongoing 'flow' of content on social and mobile media, as has been theorised by other scholars (Park & Kaye, 2020; Oeldorf-Hirsch & Srinivasan, 2022). To some extent, this may align with the 'news finds me' perception as previously discussed (see Strauß et al., 2021), as an individual approach stimulated by digitisation and social media. However, we would argue that the experience of news as 'just appearing', here, was not just confined to the expectations of certain individuals, but instead appeared as fundamental to the young adults' daily experiences of digital systems of news and information partly shaped by automation and algorithmic steering of news and information habits (cf. Antunovic et al., 2018).

Social media as a source of news

In some of the interviews and focus groups, there were spontaneous comparisons of what accessing news and information via social media more specifically involved, compared with traditional news media. Social media, here, were often held up as an important, yet different, source of news and information, useful for keeping up to date with smaller and larger events, and for easy access to fast-paced information considered relevant. They could thus be described as complementing news in traditional media, providing alternative perspectives or giving opportunities for gaining a deeper knowledge about specific events. At the time of the research, Black Lives Matter and Covid-19 were, for instance, major, ongoing news stories, and these two examples were mentioned in several of the interviews and focus groups as something that participants had attempted to learn more about through social media, for example by turning to influencers on Instagram or video-logs on YouTube to find out about specific aspects of these events. Such descriptions align with several contemporary studies of people's information practices that show that news journalism is far from the only source of information in people's lives (see Stald, 2023) and that several different kinds of media content can be seen as news (Costera Meijer & Groot Kormelink, 2015, 2020; Peters et al., 2022; Örnebring & Hellekant Rowe, 2022).

Some of the participants made a distinction between news journalism and other kinds of information, such as a group of male university students, 22 – 23 years old, who followed two public service radio channels on social media, but yet considered social media as 'only memes, pictures of people having babies and their cats, kind of', and felt it was important to keep updated by quality newspapers and other established news sources. Others made distinctions between news in social media and news journalism, not as something radically different, but as complementary genres within the broader concept of news. As just one example of how wide-ranging the discussions could become when speaking about different sources of news and information, it is worth quoting at length a discussion with Wilhelm, the 20-year-old IT-technician, Michelle, the 19-year-old currently unemployed, and Saga, an 18-year-old gymnasium student, all living in the countryside:

Interviewer: Do you access any news and if so, what kind of news?

Saga: It's very varied, basically. I hear news from the horse world, and … yes. That's what I find most interesting, and how Corona … I have also followed the American election a lot.

Interviewer: Where do you get this news?

Saga: Regarding the horse world, there is this app called Ridler, Corona and the election has been mostly TV4, they updated a lot.

Interviewer: But not social media then?

Saga: Instagram, in that case.

Michelle: Yes, I would say Instagram, that's where I get most of my information, but also as Saga said, horse news I check on Hippson's webpage because there's a lot of horse stuff, kind of.

Wilhelm: I use mostly Facebook I would say, because there I get everything from *Expressen* [a tabloid newspaper] to what a friend shares from their everyday life. I get everything I want, from news to entertainment.

Interviewer: What kind of news is it that you see on Instagram, Michelle?

Michelle: There's also a lot of horse stuff, because I follow several horse accounts and keep updated about horse competitions, especially now during Corona. So, I'm very much keeping track of the horse world.

Interviewer: Facebook is an important news media for you Wilhelm?

Wilhelm: Yes, when comparing Instagram and Facebook, I get more from Facebook. Instagram is more fun stuff, fun memes for example.

Michelle: It also depends a lot on what you follow on Instagram, I have actively chosen to follow several accounts that post a lot about horses, while Wilhelm maybe follows more entertaining accounts, and of course we end up with very different things then.

(...)

Interviewer: Are there any areas or countries or so that you are particularly interested in getting news about?

Michelle: I like Swedish news because I follow a lot of horse-news, to keep track of competitions, if they will go through with them or not. What will happen with Falsterbo Horse Show, and the Swedish Championship and so on.

Saga: I keep very much updated about the horse world in Sweden as well as internationally, I find it really interesting to hear others' points of view about Corona at the moment, and then also generally about new horse methods and stuff.

Wilhelm: For me, it's mostly [information about] job opportunities or apartments. Also news from around, but also entertainment. Both in Sweden and internationally. If you're looking for a job, it's in Sweden, but entertainment you check internationally.

Interviewer: Do you read international news in Swedish news media?

Wilhelm: It depends, but mostly English [media] I think. I don't know if it's USA's own sites, but it's different. I get different [sites/suggestions] in my news feed, it can be about Johnny Depp or other news, but it's in my feed.

Interviewer: What kind of English-language can it be?

Wilhelm: There are some vlogs, or news sites, that not only contain one thing, but a mixture of things.

(Focus group, 18–20, countryside)

This discussion clearly exemplifies the porous borders between news and other media content in the minds of these young people, and illustrates how social media platforms such as Instagram and Facebook could play a major role as providers of news and information. And even though there were of course differences among respondents, based on age as well as social class and other factors shaping news consumption, this way of seeing all kinds of content in social media as news was, in fact, common among the entire group of participants, with the two ways of understanding news, as journalism and news media, and as a much wider range of content and formats, often co-existing in the discussions. Although the young Swedes in general were familiar with the basic differences between news journalism and other mediated information integrated in their information repertoires and overall media use, such as journalists' intention, work process and ethos, these insights did not affect how they shaped their daily information practices or conceptualised news. Alongside the notion of 'news-ness' as a way to think about how news can be understood on an audience level, we could therefore also use the categories suggested in a report by the Reuters Institute of Journalism on young people and news, which, based on a qualitative study of young adults in three different countries (Brazil, the UK and US) makes a distinction between 'the news' and 'news', as a help for thinking about news from a broader perspective, where the latter entails a plethora of information that young people consider to be new, in a range of different areas (Collao, 2022, p. 15).

When describing social media as sites for news, some, furthermore, underlined how social media platforms could be valued precisely because they differed from news journalism, not least due to the availability of user-generated stories and more personal perspectives. Such accounts illustrated in our material correlate with a recent study of young Dutch smartphone users by Joëlle Swart and Marcel Broersma (2023), which points to how we might think of a difference between young people's awareness of what news is, traditionally, and their experiences of what news 'feels like', on platforms such as Instagram. One participant, who explained how she used Instagram to learn about the situation for Uyghurs in China, also emphasised how she perceived a difference in the focus of news on social media versus traditional news media, where social media, as she experienced it, could provide more attention to specific issues:

> News on social media, for me, are things that happen that aren't given so much attention in, like, *Aftonbladet* – like demonstrations. Or like the rainforest in Amazonas or fires in Australia, that wasn't written about so much in *Aftonbladet*, but it was more on Instagram.
>
> (Lovisa, 21, university student, metropolitan area)

One participant in a group of 18-year-old gymnasium students, who lived in a less affluent suburb in a metropolitan area and claimed to almost solely access news and information about society on social media, developed a similar view that social media platforms could extend knowledge about topics and perspectives that traditional news media did not cover:

> Interviewer: Which types of news do you find most interesting to get updated on?
>
> Absalon: I like to take part of news that affects me. The kind of news that I mainly see online (on social media) is to do with injustices. That's because injustices aren't shown in the same

way in traditional media, it won't get the same amount of viewings. ... About a month ago, there was news about police brutality in Nigeria. I wouldn't have known about it if I hadn't seen it online, it was only there that I could see it. It wasn't covered anywhere on, like, SVT or *Aftonbladet*.

Interviewer: Where did you get the information about the police brutality...?

Absalon: First on Twitter, cause it was trending there. Then I went in there and checked and got a lot of information. The week after I saw it everywhere on Instagram and YouTube. People were sharing it on their stories, it was everywhere.

(Absalon, 18, gymnasium student, metropolitan area)

Social media, here, are seen as more suited than traditional news media in covering certain topics of particular interest, and for gaining information about specific geographical areas not in focus in the Swedish news media. It is also clear that, as social media platforms are described as the *only* place to obtain what these young participants defined as news, different social media platforms gain different roles in shaping this, as in this example when Twitter became the first place that Absalon heard about police brutality in Nigeria, as a 'trending' topic, which he, then, would learn more about through shared stories and personal interpretations on Instagram and YouTube. In these instances, our material can clearly be compared to the news use observed by Clark and Marchi (2017) in their work with American teenagers, in highlighting a simultaneous disillusionment with 'legacy' news and the formation of alternative sources of knowledge and public engagement on social media, where Clark and Marchi are drawing on Papacharissi's (2015) notion of 'affective publics' to describe how young people become part of the news story by emotive declarations online (2017, pp. 117–119).

Influencers and memes as news genres

The experiences among participants of social media as providing a particular form of *news*, with its own news values and prioritised perspectives and responses, meant that what was considered as sources of news, finally, could also be extended to new genres – of which influencers and memes were two noteworthy categories that could be referred to as key news sources in the interviews and focus groups. Influencers – a term that was rather broadly used by the participants to refer to popular individuals with a large online following – primarily seemed to have a role in areas such as lifestyle, fashion, training and beauty, but they were also, by some, considered useful for providing information on areas such as Covid-19, Black Lives Matter or feminism, or for topics relating to politics or activism, at the same time as they could be appreciated for providing an interpretive community. The latter aspect was exemplified in the interview with Tuva, the shop assistant introduced earlier, who was particularly engaged in feminism and anti-racism, and who explained how certain influencer accounts on Instagram had become highly significant to her, as her friends were less interested in politics and she no longer had her father around to discuss these interests with:

> Interviewer: So you choose not to talk about that type of political stuff with your friends?
>
> Tuva: No, they know where I stand. But I think most of them have become bored (laughter), or aren't interested. I notice that and it's a shame, but what can I do? I used to talk a lot about it with my dad, but hardly with my mum, she's not interested. So I think that's it, to have access to someone you can communicate with about what's happening, as I don't have a lot of access to mainstream media, and before it was always dad who I could talk to.
>
> Interviewer: So these accounts, or influencers, they fill that kind of function for you?
>
> Tuva: Mm.

Here it is relevant to underline influencers as a hybrid source of 'news' shaped by what Zizi Papacharissi (2015, p. 29) and Alfred Hermida (2010) have referred to as an 'ambient' environment for news, with a potential impact on engagement in political issues as well as in the wider public sphere, while balancing between commercialism and authenticity (see Arriagada & Bishop, 2021).

The discussions about influencers and celebrities, likewise, would sometimes illustrate not only their role in providing information and how they could serve as interpretive communities – in some ways mirroring earlier forms of celebrity culture (c.f. Johansson, 2015) – but also how they would function as opinion-leaders, able to articulate political opinion and stimulate discussion. Maria, a 21-year-old care assistant, who followed several influencers and celebrity accounts on Instagram and YouTube, and who had explained that for her, the notion of 'news' entailed anything from updates from *Aftonbladet* to advice on Covid-19 from the public health authority and celebrity postings on social media, gave an example of such an instance from her daily social media feed:

> Maria: I think it was Joel Kinnaman who had posted about Black Lives Matter, saying that we're all human and the same, irrespective of the colour of our skin. And he, sort of, made an argument for that, that no one deserves that kind of injustice, and that there should be equal justice for everyone. And I really agree with that, it's really important!
>
> (Maria, 21, care assistant, mid-size town)

Social media postings by famous people, in this case a well-known Swedish actor voicing his opinion on a major news story, could, then, lead to wider reflections on politics and society, as well as providing support of one's own opinions.

Another genre that was repeatedly mentioned as an in some ways important source of information and commentary on news, outside of news journalism, was memes – humorous images or video clips with a witty caption or a short accompanying text. This type of digital content has been shown to play a significant role in global digital culture, often spreading very fast and being shaped by a multitude of users (Miltner, 2018; Shifman, 2014), with the potential for creative and participatory elements as well as for weaponizing political discourse (e. g. Denisova, 2019; Milner, 2018; Peters & Allan, 2021; Wiggins, 2019). Memes were, in this study, particularly appreciated for providing a humourous touch to the everyday. They were, by some, considered pure entertainment but could also be regarded as a way to gain – or share – information about different kinds of public issues, albeit in a light-hearted way. To take another example from the focus group with the gymnasium students quoted earlier, memes could be a way to comment on, and to add a humorous touch to, certain events or news stories:

> Absalon: I usually send memes to people, both to groups and just friends. I belong to several groups where we send memes to each other. If you take part in a discussion you can send a relevant meme that everyone understands. Different memes suit different people, so that's why I send memes to different people, depending on if I think that they will like them or not.

> Interviewer: Where do you find the memes, then?

> Absalon: People make memes as soon as anything happens, so there are always memes on Instagram, at least for me. I follow a lot of meme accounts, but there are lots of memes on general accounts too. A lot on Twitter too – those are the best ones! There aren't as many as on Instagram there, but they're more true to reality. There are a lot of videos there, so I usually download them and then pass them along.

> Interviewer: By 'true to reality', do you mean that they are relatable?

> Absalon: Yeah, exactly. For example, yesterday, everyone wanted to cancel Kevin Hart [an actor]. So then there were a lot of memes about Kevin Hart, that he's short and things like that, it was funny. But different memes are fun for different people.

Absalon, who took considerable care choosing suitable memes for his friends, exemplifies how, for some of the young adults, memes could form an important part of the social activities of groups and smaller communities on social media, allowing particular individuals to take on a dominant role in curating and distributing these. Although memes were generally not described as news, they could clearly be used as vehicles for information about society, politics and popular culture, with potential to engage and provide the basis for identification and experiences of belonging among members of smaller groups. Such small groups, further, may be seen as a form of 'micro-public', "permitting the circulation of information, ideas and debates in an unfettered manner" (Clark & Marchi, 2017, p. 116), while small groups formed around messaging apps and social media, furthermore, can be seen as important spaces for maintaining 'public connection', as a social practice potentially orienting people towards public life (Swart et al., 2018, cf. Couldry et al., 2007a, 2007b). In the same way as influencers, or, indeed, podcasts, video-logs and many other digital media genres, can be regarded as important sources of news and information for young people, so, too, did these discussions exemplify how the uses of social media as platforms for news, as described by the participants, necessitate a continued renewed analysis not only of the concept of news, but also of what it can entail for young people.

Conclusion

In this chapter, we have discussed how young people can encounter and come into contact with news as part of their highly digitised day-to-day lives, and, crucially, within their broader media use. As shown by earlier research on the role of news in everyday life, to gain a nuanced understanding of this it is important to acknowledge how news consumption is embedded into overall media practices, which, for the young adults in this study, were primarily linked to digital media, with smartphones a key device for news and information, and social media providing a dominant framework for their engagement with different kinds of media content and information throughout the day. Although being an informed citizen was generally seen as an ideal, correlating to previous research on young news audiences, news did initially not appear to be highly prioritised as part of the range of available formats and content, with a slight discrepancy between ideas of what one *should* do, and the accounts of what a 'media day' would *actually* involve. Despite this, many different sources of news and information were incorporated into the young adults' varied and fluid media use, ranging from TV news programmes to news apps and a variety of news and information in social media. While preferences for news journalism could differ, many seemed to prefer easily accessible and entertaining news content for regular news updates and for engaging content, as for instance found in a tabloid news app or on a morning news show, or to be able to get quick overviews of headlines and brief news stories, with the price also mentioned as a factor that could determine which news source to access online.

The chapter has also begun to highlight the porous boundaries between news and social media in the eyes of a young audience, illustrating how social media can be integrated into their lives as major, and sometimes the only, sources of news, experienced not just as networking platforms for the distribution of news journalism, but also as carrying other kinds of content that could, for many, relatively

seamlessly be experienced as 'news'. Such content could be regarded as a complement to news journalism, allowing for different perspectives on news stories and
more personal content, but social media platforms were also described as valued
for providing radically different kinds of 'news' compared with traditional news
media, and as operating from within a different set of news values altogether.
As such, the notion of social media as providers of news directs analytical attention to novel 'news' categories or sources, of which user-generated content, influencers and memes came across as examples of important sources of news and information outside of news journalism, with particular consequences for the
formation of 'affective-' and 'micro-publics', which we will discuss further later
in this book.

Finally, this first look at our research participants' daily encounters with news
and information has emphasised not only the routinised and mundane aspects of
these, but also how news and other types of information can appear, to a young
audience, as part of an automated flow, with the notion of news as 'just appearing'
underlined in the chapter. This aspect of the young adults' news consumption,
which partly relates to processes of automation and an algorithmic selection of
content on social media, came across as significant as part of the overall experiences of digital systems of news and information, and, alongside many of the other
initial findings that have been presented here, is something that fruitfully can be
returned to for an extended analysis.

Chapter 4
Practices, interests and new news categories

As we saw in the previous chapter, 'news', as perceived in a broad way, is encountered and made meaningful in a wide variety of technological environments and can be understood as originating from different formats and sources. This means that the concept of news, in some ways, is disintegrating, as the distribution of news is spread over a wide variety of platforms, and that using news is a practice that has undergone significant changes during the last decades. In this chapter, we will take a closer look at the everyday news practices of the young adults: the different ways in which news, as our participants define it, is integrated into everyday life, but also how it is made meaningful in these practices. Starting from an analysis of the varied ways that news, as stemming both from traditional news media and from a range of other sources, is incorporated into the broader practice of media use in everyday life, we will move on to take a look at the young adults' preferred news subjects, relating it also to what news topics young adults were interested in taking part of in previous media landscapes. Lastly, we will further discuss the ways the young adults conceptualise news, in their own way, and what this means.

Underlying the focus of the chapter is the notion of 'media practice' (Couldry, 2004, 2012), following a long line of scholarship inspired by anthropological theory and method (c.f. Bird 2010) as a way to highlight the significance of both what people say about media and what they 'do' with media, including how a range of media content and technologies are integrated in routines and activities beyond the engagement with content alone, including its material and spatiotemporal aspects. As we saw in the previous chapter, the young adults encountered news in a variety of intentional and unintentional ways and in varied contexts, and their news use was interlinked with a diverse media use as well as deeply integrated in other everyday life practices, which will be further analysed here. In the first part of this chapter, we will present three different spatiotemporal ways in which news was used and made meaningful in the lives of the young adults: 1) interval news practices, 2) synchronal news practices and 3) ritual news practices. As ideal types, these categories are mutually exclusive, although this was not necessarily the case in everyday practice. In the following, we will, after a brief discussion of current scholarship relating to the spatiotemporal dimensions of news use, describe these three ways of engaging with 'news', and then move on to discuss how these practices can be linked to the broader role of news and meaning-making in the young adults' lives.

'News' practices in everyday life

Transformed news formats and practices have during the last decades sparked a growing scholarly interest in the way news interweaves with audiences' everyday lives, and how sense-making practices around news are situated socially, culturally and experientially. A practice approach to media can be combined with our approach to news, as it often uses ethnographic methods, and calls for a broad approach to a situated understanding of media use, as contextually, culturally and socially anchored. One main advantage with this perspective is that it is broader than, but also includes, text–audience relations, which here means we are not bound by any specific sort of news (news journalism, social media, influencers, etc.) and thus can focus on the news practices in the full information practices of the young adults. Looking at news as an everyday practice takes a broad grip on news in its context and, as formulated by Couldry, focuses on the full range of practices oriented towards media (not just direct media consumption) (Couldry, 2004, 2012).

According to Kristin van Damme et al. (2015) the context of news consumption is divided into three strongly coinciding levels: time, space and social context (see also Costera Meijer & Groot Kormelink, 2015; Groot Kormelink & Costera Meijer, 2020). The temporal and spatial dimensions of news consumption in particular have gained some heightened attention lately, revealing how and why the widening agency in appropriating various places and social spaces in everyday life relates to general news media consumption. Broersma and Peters (2013) have, for example, shown how digital news use becomes less centred around fixed places, times and patterns of everyday life, and John Dimmick et al. (2011) discussed how news is used in the interstices in time (also Van Damme et al., 2015, p. 208). Earlier research on news consumption and time has tended to place a premium on the speed of news production, distribution and consumption (Phillips, 2012), however Keightley's and Downey's (2018) analysis of the temporal dimensions of news consumption, introduced in Chapter 2, stresses how this is constituted through an interplay between mediated and socially constructed time, interlinking with multiple temporalities in everyday experience. Peters (2012), similarly, has said that "space matters for how we experience journalism and (…) how we experience journalism shapes our social spaces" (p. 701; cf. Schrøder, 2015, p. 74) and suggests that space has a particular phenomenological meaning for news consumption in digital culture as "the emerging technologies and increasingly mobile spatialities of journalism do more than just replicate news content – by changing the public's experience of journalistic consumption, they change what news is" (Peters, 2012, p. 701). In this chapter we will take a closer look at how these new news practices change what news means, and how they relate to the broader world according to our young participants.

When asked to talk freely about their uses of media and information in everyday life, as explained in the discussion of research methods in Chapter 2, the young adults in general described how they spent a substantial amount of time with different kinds of social media, in combination with podcasts, TV series, documentaries and news journalism, echoing the same kind of broad information repertoires that Peters et al. highlighted (2022) and which we started to outline in Chapter 3 where we also paid attention to their more automated news consumption. Despite this, the media use of different individuals varied, due to factors such as age, lifestyle, occupation and socioeconomic background, forming different combinations where varied kinds of media co-existed and were meaningful in different ways in their lives. As underlined also by previous research (Boczkowski et al., 2018; Bengtsson & Johansson, 2022), different technologies interplay and form diverse platforms for the distribution of news, necessitating a holistic approach to the 'media life' (Deuze, 2012) of young people. Discussions about news and information practices in everyday life, hence, often turned into a rather messy discussion about a great variety of practices, media formats and content, relating to the structure of the ordinary day and when and where different types of media were integrated into it.

Interval news practices

The most common way to talk about news use in general among the young adults was, in fact, to down-play its significance in the structure of the day, as also noted in Chapter 3. This was primarily done by negating the idea of a fixed and focused time and space devoted to news (cf. Broersma & Peters, 2013), but also, in relation to news journalism, to talk about this as a minor part of their overall media use, which did not always come up initially in the spontaneous descriptions of a 'media day'. As seen in the previous chapter, too, a common way that the young adults used news was to just pick up the phone when they had nothing else to do, when a gap in time appeared. Dimmick et al. (2011) have identified this temporal aspect of news use in digital media, showing that news today is often consumed in the interstices of time. Our interviews and focus groups reveal a similar approach to news, following from its heavy integration in media use in general. News, therefore, as part of the broader fabric of media use, was often used to fill empty timeslots: while waiting for the train, sitting on the bus, standing in a line or waiting for the toast to pop up from the toaster: a kind of *interval use*. Penelope (19), working in a preschool during her 'gap year', exemplified this aspect of news use:

I rarely think: 'now I'm gonna get on Instagram to keep myself updated about world events. It's more like I check what's happening, what people do, and just scroll for a bit because I've nothing better to do, I'm just waiting.

(Penelope, 19, childcare assistant, metropolitan area)

These interstices in time take place in spaces that one does not know the exact length of, they are too short to watch an episode of a TV series or a film and are hence temporally fluid. The only media content that can be practised in a meaningful way in such situations is really short posts in social media, such as for instance TikTok videos, and short notifications from news journalism. The participants described it as a kind of un-reflected use, where the content is subordinate to the purpose of killing time or keeping loneliness away, in many ways mirroring what has been found in previous audience research emphasising how media habits often relate more to the requirements of the everyday situation than the particular content (c.f. Bausinger, 1984; Morley, 1986). A presumption of engagement in news has also been questioned in research looking at how engagement and attention relate to time spent with news, showing that both brief and longer periods of time spent can be unrelated to interest or attention (Kormelink & Costera Meijer, 2020). This kind of interval use is, furthermore, experienced as tech-independent; it is not important which platform one uses in the temporal interstices – instead it is meaningful as a way to resist monotony and social emptiness, often involving 'scrolling', which has been described in another study of digital news consumption as "a strong, embodied urge to keep up the movement of the hand" (Kormelink & Costera Meijer, 2019, p. 650). Some participants used these intervals to actively go through a news app such as a quick visit to a main news site of a tabloid newspaper or public service television, while others stayed with broader social media apps such as Instagram or TikTok and just received 'the news' and other sorts of information that was shown in their news feeds.

Some of the young adults described such interval news use, dealing primarily with temporal and social vacuums in everyday life, as their main way to stay informed about the world, relating closely to the 'news finds me' perception identified by Homero Gil De Zúñiga et al. (2017) and introduced in Chapter 3, as something particularly significant among young participants. De Zúñiga and colleagues (2020) have shown that younger people (18–35 years of age) demonstrate much higher levels of NFM compared with older age groups (p. 1624). This may also be due to the fact that such spatiotemporal organisation of news use requires a life characterised by a high level of spatiotemporal flexibility. Many young adults lead such lives in Sweden today, compared with older adults: the youngest go to the gymnasium, with relatively high levels of flexibility in the organisation of time and space; one-third of all young adults are students in higher education and have an even more notable spatiotemporal freedom to organise their lives. Interval news use was more difficult to uphold for those among the young participants that led more 'adult lives', working full-time, in workplaces that demanded their full attention. For Penelope, the care assistant quoted above, social media use during work hours was strictly forbidden:

> I usually work between eight to four, and then I don't use my phone or media at all. But on my way to work I'm on the bus for around 35 minutes, and then I go through everything. Instagram, Facebook, Snapchat (...). After that I don't use the phone during the day, maybe just checking the time or sending an sms if it's important. On the bus on my way back home I sit with my phone for 30 minutes and do the same thing as in the morning, checking what's going on, what people are posting, if something has happened.
>
> (Penelope, 19, childcare assistant, metropolitan area)

Beatrice (25), a biochemistry student at the university in a big city who at the time of the interview had a summer job as a laboratory assistant, had also witnessed how her adult working life changed her social media news habits:

> Now when I'm working, 8–5, kind of, we're not allowed to use our mobiles in the lab. I can only check the phone when I go to the toilet or during a break. So, my phone use has gone down, drastically. And I also ride my bike to work so I can't do lazy commuter surfing anymore.
>
> (Beatrice, 25, university student, metropolitan area)

It is hence contextually dependent how the empty slots in daily life are organised, and heavy practice of interval news use was more common among those who adhered to a typical youth-oriented lifestyle, with lots of flexibility and temporal independence.

Synchronal news practices

Interval news use is closely related to the next kind of information practice: synchronal news practices. Previous research has noticed that it can be a challenge for young people to be informed about the world and current affairs as they get a large proportion of their news incidentally, *when they are doing something else online* (see Van Damme et al., 2020; Westlund & Bjur, 2013; De Zúñiga et al., 2017; Stald, 2023).

As we saw in the earlier discussion about interval news practices, many of the young adults described how they spent a substantial amount of time with social media on an ordinary day, and how these media played important roles as information providers for them (along many other important purposes, see Bengtsson

& Johansson, 2022). It was obvious that different kinds of social media platforms were used side by side and fulfilled different roles, which also varied according to age, gender and socioeconomic background, and between individuals. As underlined also by Boczkowski et al. (2018), different platforms were used in different ways and played different roles, although most social media were used for broad and varied purposes by many of the young adults. Facebook was for example used for purposes such as following interest groups, taking part in family networks and finding information about specific restaurants, but was also a source of information about local events, traffic works in the area and traditional news journalism. Twitter (now X) was not only a way to follow discussions about current affairs but was also mentioned by many as an important entertainment platform, putting forward memes as one important reason to be on Twitter. Instagram was for many a particularly important platform for keeping one's social life together, and a source of inspiration about food, home decoration and fashion, but where one would also find news in a traditional sense, as posts from traditional news providers, or shared by people in one's networks.

Another way of using news was hence as a *synchronal*, a parallel, activity, used simultaneously with other everyday tasks or in parallel with other media practices. This could be conducted accidentally as part of one's broader social media use, but also more intentionally for the purpose of, for example, feeling less lonely. Such practices could be to keep TikTok or YouTube on while preparing food, scrolling Instagram when eating (on your own) or before going to bed. This might hence be seen as another category of interval use, where the interval is social instead of temporal. Letting social media fill an empty gap in life, when someone, according to our social norms and conventions, should have been there, such as during mealtimes, is a way of ordering everyday situations when living, or being, alone. Lovisa (20), who had left her hometown to study political science at the university in a big city, used YouTube in this way as a routine practice while for example preparing dinner:

> I mainly go on YouTube to pass the time, and sometimes I have vlogs and stuff like that on the computer just in the background, because I've got nothing to do. Like when cooking or doing something like that.
>
> (Lovisa, 20, university student, metropolitan area)

August (18), a gymnasium student still living with his parents in a mid-sized town, regularly used YouTube for the same purpose while having breakfast:

> I check YouTube a lot on my mobile, because it's so easy to bring along and watch at the same time. So, as soon as I wake up I put on a video, which I watch while I have breakfast. I don't

know why I do it, but I use [social media] almost too much maybe, all the time. ... Because I always want something on.

(August, 18, gymnasium student, mid-sized town)

Synchronal news use, as is clear from these examples, is as it was described in our sample, more oriented towards less traditional 'news' than news journalism. It could include content such as social media posts from news organisations, but also from influencers, NGOs or other organisations, just as some of the young adults used to have the TV news on while having breakfast.

Ritual news practices

While both interval and synchronal news use were often put forward by the young adults as the most immediate description of their information practices, when we asked for a more detailed description of their daily habits around news and information another picture emerged, revealing a distinctively different way of approaching 'news' compared with the liquidity of both synchronal and interval use: news use as an everyday ritual. Ritual news practices were particularly underlined when talking about morning rituals, about starting the day, described as a systematic, conscious, and spatiotemporally delimited media practice. Nathalie (19), a woman in a group of currently unemployed friends living in the countryside outside a mid-sized town, explained how she used social media in the morning (and evening):

> The first thing I do when I wake up is to go on TikTok, and then I might stay there for half an hour, then I go on Instagram for half an hour, then Snapchat for half an hour. Then I have like an hour and a half to wake up. I guess it's a routine that I have almost every day, apart from the weekend.
>
> M: So, there's a certain order...?
>
> Yes, and before I go to bed I also go through all the three social media that I have. So, it's like a routine, in the morning and in the evening.
>
> (Nathalie, 19, unemployed, countryside)

Nathalie's account, humorously recognised by her friends in the group, also emphasised the perceived importance of social media for catching up with what had happened during the night, when one had been sleeping and cut off from the flow of information and social events, something which was also repeated by other respondents. Pierre (18), a gymnasium student living in a less affluent metropolitan suburb, had a similar way of organising his morning routines:

> The first thing you see when you wake up are the notifications. I start the app with the most notifications. I hardly have time to wake up before I'm on Shapchat and start scrolling and checking who's written to me. After I've been on Snapchat I go on Instagram and scroll quickly, and then I check if I've had any messages there.
>
> (Pierre, 18, gymnasium student, metropolitan area)

One of our older participants, Lily (24), who worked in the local assembly in the small town where she lived, gave an elaborate description of her media morning ritual, talking about how she lay in bed, drinking coffee that her fiancé had brought her, a fixed time slot that lasted for half an hour while she took part in the latest happenings and updates on social media:

> Well, my partner wakes me up before he's going to work. So, he wakes me up around half past eight. With coffee! And then I just have to stay in bed, haha. (...) I do it every morning. And I check my mail, and if I've had an sms I reply. I check Facebook, check my work's Facebook. Well, I just scan everything, for around half an hour, I guess.
>
> (Lily, 24, assembly assistant, mid-sized town)

Some also portrayed a similar ritualistic media use in the evenings, that was likewise used to end the day, before going to sleep and closing off the world. This ritual information practice is profoundly different compared with both interval and synchronal use, and the NFM identified by Gil de Zúñiga et al. (2017; 2020). Everyday transformations, such as this 'news' ritual, are temporally and spatially fixed, provide stability and take place in a specific place (in fact often in bed) and during a specific time (from when one wakes up in the morning, and a delimited time from there) and hence are essential in starting the day for the young adults. Ritual news practices also differs from interval and synchronal use as it is tech-specific, as our participants described in detail which platforms they went through and often also in what specific order. It is furthermore transitional in character; it transforms the respondents from uninformed sleepers to updated social creatures ready to meet a new day. In this sense it has a lot in common with earlier rituals of news use, as described by Bausinger (1984) and Larsen (2000) (see also Berelson, 1948).

Old and new news interests

As will be further elaborated on in Chapter 5, and as has also been noticed by other studies, many of the young participants put forward one, or a small number of topics in which they were particularly interested. This was something that came up unprompted in the interviews and focus groups, but that we started to notice along the way of the fieldwork. These topics were often described as societal issues of a more structural character, sometimes, but not always, of great urgency, but seldom framed as relating to specific events. Such topics could be the climate crisis, feminism, racism, LGBTQ+ issues or similar areas. Stald (2023) reports related findings from a larger Danish study of young news consumers, which revealed that most young Danes "are interested in and have strong opinions about the larger issues such as human interest topics, climate, environment and sustainability, or the large-scale consequences of the pandemic, while they fluctuate between different causes, according to the current newsfeeds and inputs from friends and family" (Stald, 2023, p. 283).

The young Swedes in this study also often highlighted one, or maybe a few, larger structural issues that they found particularly interesting and wanted to stay informed about. They looked eagerly for information about these issues, and often engaged in anything they could find about 'their' specific topic: social media posts, news journalism locally, nationally and internationally, podcasts, documentaries, and so on. We call these deeply essential, and structural, interests '*my-topics*', as they were also discussed by our participants as something that defined them as human beings, important aspects of their identity and their cultural boundary work, something which is particularly emphasised when one is young and more heavily involved in an intense identity process. These 'my-topics' resonate well with what Clark and Marchi (2017) identified as 'connective journalism', that we discussed in Chapter 1. Connective journalism, they mean, is journalism about topics that young people care about enough to engage in, by searching for information, but also sharing the information with others, and hence contributing to shaping the story. In their efforts to share and create this news, young people hence insert themselves into the story. Just like the findings we have presented in this book, connective journalism is broader than just news journalism, and includes many other media formats. Connective journalism has much in common with the 'my-topics' that we identified, as they also revolve around broader societal structures. 'My-topics' were also interesting to the young adults beyond proximity in time and space: it did not matter whether they related to something that happened in a remote place, or long ago – if they related to the young person's specific interest, or were of interest to someone they knew, they were considered to be important information anyway.

In order to understand the 'window on the world' (Tuchman, 1978, p. 1) that young people are looking through in today's digitised and fragmented media landscape, we asked specifically about what topics the young adults made sure they were informed about, were interested in following and being updated about, and paid attention to within their daily media practices. Besides the exclusive my-topics, of particularly strong interest, the topics that they put forward were recognisable and often profoundly mundane, and resonate well with what we know from earlier news research. It is of course difficult to do justice to the breadth of the areas they included in their media use, but when painting a picture of this, certain areas of interest summarise what kind of information the young adults were *generally* interested in being updated about.

The first category is *things that happen in my local area and/or affect me (or the people in my networks) personally.* This category includes mundane aspects such as what the weather will be like, if public transport works adequately, or if (during the state of the pandemic) my university course or workplace has gone online. Such information provides hands-on information about practical things that it is necessary to know in order to function properly in everyday life: to have proper clothing, to bring an umbrella, or make adjustments to be on time for class or work. The second category is *things that happen to friends and acquaintances*, which means staying informed of what close friends and family are up to, including micro-dimensions about everything from what the people in the young adults' networks are doing on their vacation, to larger life-events: if a friend or an old acquaintance has got married, got a new job, got a new baby, or if one's old school-teacher has died. The third category is information about *public events in my local area.* Even though a majority of our interviews were conducted during the pandemic, the young adults still talked and dreamed about taking part in public live events in the place where they lived: concerts, film and music festivals, public lectures or other things of interest. Related to this, but also a bit easier to maintain during the pandemic, was information about *entertainment* in a broader sense: which new TV series to keep an eye on, new interesting podcasts in their areas of interests, newly released music, as well as films, literature, and so on. Some participants were also eagerly following information about sports. This included information about their favourite football or ice hockey clubs, ongoing contests, games, updates about results or information about sports celebrities. The fifth category is *other people's opinions.* This means they wanted to know about other people's ideas, not just the mere facts describing an event (an aspect of the young adults' news practices and perceptions which will be further developed in Chapter 6). The last among the areas of interest that we identify here, that also most closely resembles traditional news journalism, is *things that happen in the broader world.* This category included information about events outside of their own local area and areas of particular interest, which concerned people other than themselves and the people that they know.

As we have already discussed in Chapter 3, the young adults received information about these areas of interest through a mixture of digital and analogue media, for example influencers, ads and friends, as well as news journalism. On the one hand this underlines the novel aspects of contemporary news use, yet these areas of interest are very familiar. Sports, entertainment, ads, and local and global events are, after all, what newspapers have been filled with for as long as we can remember, with earlier research on news audiences likewise showing how categories such as gossip and opinion can be of an equal standing to current affairs in the overall news experience (e.g. Williams, 1962; Bird, 1997; Johansson, 2007). Costera Meijer and Groot Kormelink (2020), in synthesising studies they conducted with university students over several decades, conclude, as noted in the introductory chapter, that although young people's news practices have changed since the early 2000s, their *experiences* of using news have remained largely the same during the same time period, appearing to indicate that it is rather how and where the information is provided that has changed, rather than people's news interests. Following this suggestion, historic sources can provide points of reference about how young people made sense of 'the news' in previous media landscapes, for example a detailed analysis of reader patterns in local newspapers conducted in Sweden 50 years ago, that looked at what people of different genders and age groups *actually read* in their local newspaper. This study showed that, of what young people (15–24 years old) read in the daily local paper in the 1970s, the most read genres were *entertainment* (read by 26%), followed by *radio/TV* (read by 24%). The next category was *family news* (read by 15%) and *sports* (read by 10%). Next came *news* (current affairs) (read by 9%) (Weibull, 1983, p. 372). Another historic point of reference is Raymond Williams's 1962 book *Communications* (1962), which presents an analysis of the distribution of news categories in British newspapers in the early 1960s. This shows that the proportion of advertising in the most common papers ranged from approximately 30—50% (Williams, 1962/1966, p. 36), while the proportion of sports content in the daily newspapers differed from 23% (*The Times*) to 43% (*The Herald*) (1962/1966, p. 43). Williams also revealed that when looking at the proportion of "political, social and economic news, both international and domestic" of the total newspapers, the figures in the general newspapers ranged from around 16% for *The Times* and *The Guardian*, to the lowest figure of about 5% in *The Sketch*. Although the percentages had risen in 1965, these numbers still point to the small amount of content in newspapers that in previous times were about current affairs news, leading Williams to conclude that "these are quite startling figures, by comparison with our usual assumptions about our main functions of our newspapers" (1962/1966, p. 43).

Williams's historic content analysis does not tell us anything about how people actually made sense of the material they met in their daily newspaper in the 1960s, and it is, of course, not meaningful to compare a qualitative phenomenological analysis about news perceptions and practices conducted in the early 2020s with a content analysis of newspapers in the 1960s, or a quantitative analysis of newspaper readers conducted in the 1970s. Yet, the overlap between the areas of interest that the young adults in our study expressed and the kinds of content that young people in the 1970s cared to read about in the local newspaper, says something about the interests of young people across time and may help us reflect upon how we interpret the practices, interests and connections of contemporary media audiences.

New news categories

A last aspect of the transforming dimensions of meaning-making around news that we will discuss in this chapter is the way the young adults talked about, and categorised, news. As mentioned in Chapter 3, Reuters Institute for the study of journalism (2022) has, in its studies, identified a new way of talking about news among young people, where '*news*', a wide category of information, was distinguished from '*the news*', which then meant traditional news journalism, something which goes well in line with how our participants also conceptualised news. The entangled mix of different kinds of media content that our participants encountered in everyday life was incorporated into everyday practices where no particular information provider turned out as *in general* more important than any other, unless something of specific urgency occurred, such as a crisis, an accident or other kinds of critical events, when most of the young adults said they would turn to established news journalism, often public service broadcasting. As also noted in Chapter 3, there was a general understanding of the basic differences between journalism and other mediated information, yet these insights were however not always taken into account, either when they shaped their daily information habits, or when conceptualising what news is.

Even though the difference between 'the news' and other kinds of news did not serve as a vital factor of distinction when navigating the media landscape, some participants articulated distinctions between, for example, news in social media and news journalism, not as something radically different, but as different genres within the broader concept of news. Penelope, for instance, meant that:

> What is different on Instagram is that news there is more personal, things that happen in people's private lives, or work lives, or something like that. That's different from when you read about the presidential election in the US, or the Corona crisis in the world. There are different kinds of news, and in social media news are often more positive.
>
> Interviewer: Can you exemplify?
>
> For example, when someone is having a baby, or have gotten a new job, or finished an education or ... Well just more personal, fun, achievements in life, kind of.
> (Penelope, 19, childcare assistant, metropolitan area)

Just as Penelope did, it was common among the interviewees to talk about information they received from social media as *news*, just another kind, but beyond news journalism. A young woman who studied sociology in a university town, Hanna, was strongly engaged in societal issues and used a great variety of different sources to keep updated about what was going on in the world. Hanna said that Instagram was the medium that she would miss the most if it disappeared, as that would disconnect her from her entire social world, including information about urgent issues that was not covered by news journalism, as well as information about acquaintances she hardly ever sees but who are part of her personal history and that she would not want to lose connection to; indicating that "the kind of news you get from there" was more essential for her as a human being, than anything she found in traditional news media.

Just as with the example of Hanna above, the young adults' construction of 'news' meant they both challenged the taken-for-granted role of news journalism and established new distinctions between different categories within the broader notion of news. An often-mentioned distinction that came up spontaneously in the interviews was that between *big* or *world news*, referring to large journalistic news events, and *smaller 'news'* – events and issues which affected the young adults and the local area where they lived (or in other ways were connected to) more directly. Smaller news was also sometimes conceptualised as *'my-news'*. Big/world news was, the young adults meant, often (but not always) provided by news journalism while small 'news' was generally provided by groups and other media producers (e. g., influencers, friends, activists or organisations) in social media.

The distinction between big/world news and my/small news to some extent reminds us of the well-known division in news journalism between *global/national* and *local* news, but the distinction between big/world news and my/small news was not simply related to geographical proximity, but also to both existential and experiential proximity, and therefore confirms, but also challenges, what earlier research has concluded about the importance of geo-cultural closeness in what makes news relevant (Schrøder, 2019) and its role as identity-related boundary work (Martin, 2008). There were variations among the young adults, as some of them considered it important to be informed about 'big news', at times referring to the shame of being caught with ignorance of such events by others, something which has been discussed before in Nordic research about news consumption as a citizen duty (Hagen, 1992, 1994; Bengtsson, 2007), while other participants had no such qualms. And, while being updated about big/world news was by some seen as a social and civic duty, small news was by basically all of them considered to be information they needed for conducting and managing their own everyday lives. Sometimes this distinction was formulated as one between big/world news and 'relevant information', where being updated about big/world news was seen as a civic duty, whereas 'relevant information' was considered relevant for navigating their own lives.

The distinction between big/world news and small (or relevant) 'news' also frequently appeared in discussions about the nuisance of news journalism: when news was discussed as an intruder in everyday life. "I don't care to read about all the shit that happens", as Elias, 23, an unemployed man, exclaimed, explaining that he considered it "a privilege of social media" to be able to reject "depressing news". This way of thinking about news also reveals a tension among the young adults between those who saw news journalism as in general important, and those who meant news journalism just obscured what was *really* important. For the latter group, social media were considered meaningful because they kept them updated only about the big news events that were shared – and hence considered worth taking part in – by the people in their social networks, whereas news events that was *not* shared and/or discussed by the people in their social media feeds was not considered worth knowing about anyway (cf. Schrøder, 2015). This underlines Schutz and Luckmann's claim that themes and topics introduced by our fellow-men are of greater importance to us (1973, p. 190), compared with those which come from unknown others, also indicating why information spread in social media, by friends, acquaintances and by influencers that could have been followed over a longer period, sometimes years, is considered more important, and paid more attention to, than content provided by anonymous, or unfamiliar, journalists and news organisations.

The distinction between 'news' that is relevant to me and 'the news' that is relevant to the world, and its connected ideas of 'news-ness' (Edgerly & Vraga, 2020a, 2020b), was not constructed in the same way by all our participants. The distinction between 'news' and 'the news', however, often framed 'the news' as, although important, revolving around a world far from one's own. Wilhelm, the IT-technician we have met before, formulated this distinction as:

> News is something that affects you, like the corona virus that affects us all. Other things that don't affect you as much can also be news, but that's important to the rest of the world.
> (Wilhelm, 20, IT technician, countryside)

The distinction between news that is relevant to me (small news) and news that is relevant to the world (big news) shows the significance of relating news to one's own personal life and situation, when distinguishing between different kinds of news. The Covid-19 pandemic is an example of 'big news' which transgresses this distinction by being important both to the individual and to the world. At the end of this discussion, we may conclude that among the young Swedish adults, 'the news' was not generally considered more important or newsworthy than 'news' as part of one's everyday habits, although many found it legitimate and highly important from a societal point of view. Carl, a 23-year-old student of game design, indicated that big news events, exemplified by accidents or terror attacks, were only newsworthy for him if they affected him personally:

> I only care about the big attacks if they affect me personally. And when people describe what has happened in social media, I don't see why they would lie about someone getting shot at … say Sergel's square. And in that way it can be good to know, that I should stay away from there for a while. Besides that, I actually don't care.
>
> (Carl, 23, university student, metropolitan area)

Conclusion

In our analysis of the young adults' news practices, we have identified three distinctive ways of integrating news in everyday practices that are spatiotemporally different, but also different in how they relate to technological diversity, the role of the content provided and the way it relates to the broader fabric of everyday life. Even though these identified ways of using news are ideal types of news practices, and hence not well-defined practices that are necessarily distinct in daily life, they direct attention to the different roles news holds in everyday life, and the purposes for using it. We have already touched upon the similarities between the transformative morning and evening rituals around the broader use of 'news' and the rituals of news journalism identified by previous research in analogue media landscapes. Even though the young adults generally did not prioritise news journalism when discussing their overall media use, their ritual 'news' practices have deepseated similarities with previous forms of news use, but also some fundamental differences. Just as rituals, in their anthropological sense, are characterised by formalised habits, practised in a specific order and with a certain transgressive meaning (Bourdieu, 1991; Couldry, 2005; Turner, 1966), getting updated about what has happened during the night is a temporally and spatially restricted practice, conducted in a specific place with specific attributes, and is conducted in an ordered manner. Along with analogue news rituals, this way of using social media is transformative, and holds a cultural meaning from an everyday life perspective. Many aspects differ between traditional news rituals and the ritual of news use across social media platforms; the kind of content provided, the news values, the sources, senders and styles of communication. But from a broader audience perspective these two practices to some extent serve a need for relevant *updates* about the world, as a way of getting ready to meet the new day. Ritual media use may in this sense, and in line with how analogue news rituals have been understood, hold a transformation from private to public space, but the social media rituals that our participants described in general aimed at updating them about the current state of the people and the topics discussed in their personal networks, and therefore mark a transformation from an individual to a relational state, rather than a transformation from private to public space, marking a fundamental difference in the role of news in connecting people to the world.

Interval use of news is different from ritual news practice in spatiotemporal terms, as it is not restricted in time and space but takes place in micro-temporal interstices in everyday life – even though a common experience among our participants was also that temporal intervals can expand and occupy much more time than initially intended. This way of using news is meaningful as a continuous update of existing information, including information and updates provided by friends and family. Interval news use involves updating oneself on ongoing events and information about the people in one's networks, and is important for keeping connected to close others, friends and family, as well as, for some, to the broader world.

Synchronal news use on the one hand referred to how the young adults encountered both 'news' and 'the news' in new and multifaceted formats, but on the other hand also referred to habitually using news simultaneously with other everyday practices, such as listening to podcasts while walking to school or at the gym, watching a documentary while eating, or getting updates from a favourite YouTuber when brushing one's teeth. We know from earlier research that this way of using news is not new, as it is integrated into the fabric of the everyday. Contemporary digital and mobile media, however, have intensified these practices, by facilitating a highly mobile and flexible media use, also mixing news content to a much higher degree with other media content than was the case in previous media landscapes.

When turning our gaze from these everyday practices to the media content that the young people were interested in, we see the same mixture of novelties and continuities compared with previous media use patterns. When looking at what areas the young adults we spoke to said they were interested in getting information about, there are many similarities with previous news use, as the identified areas of interest of the young adults in contemporary Sweden, for example, to a large extent appear to be largely similar to the parts of local daily newspapers that young adults in Sweden read in the 1970s. This implies that if we consider 'news' to be broader than 'the news', the changes that we and other researchers see in user patterns and preferences for formats and sources do not immediately suggest a decline in the interests in the *topics* of news. At least not if we consider, as has been shown by for example Raymond Williams (1962), that newspapers previously covered many other areas of interest, besides current affairs news. A possible conclusion may instead be that social, and other digital, media today fulfil the same request for information that traditional newspapers used to do, only richer and providing a more direct user agency, as media users today to a larger extent choose the kind of information in which they want to engage.

Departing from this, yet another (provocative) idea comes forward: we often hear that the audience has abandoned 'the news', but the above rather indicates that is not the audience that has changed, and has become less interested in news, but rather the way news and information is produced, packaged, provided and spread. We do get richer and more detailed information today about friends and acquaintances' new jobs, weddings, babies and deaths from social media than from the family pages in newspapers, even if we subscribe to a local newspaper. Football clubs provide their fans with much more and deeper information about teams, matches, injuries, and strategies via their own webpages, blogs, posts in social media, and so on than news journalism can possibly do. TV series and films are accessed via the Netflix or HBO app, and local events reach their audiences via social media – as does news journalism. One way of thinking about this is, hence, that the audience has followed the content in which they are interested to the places where it is provided in the best, and richest, way. In the next chapter we will take a closer look at what makes 'news' as well as 'the news' considered relevant by our young participants.

Chapter 5
Why 'news' matters

In his study of rumours as an alternative kind of news, Tamotsu Shibutani (1966) claimed that news is not just information, but "information that is important to someone" (p. 40). Building his sociological theory on the study of a large number of rumours, he underscored that people gather and search for information about matters that are urgent for them. From such a perspective it is not surprising that one of the core aspects that spontaneously emerged in the discussions with our participants was the *relevance* of news, emphasising that news needs to be important, or to some extent useful, for people to bother to pay attention to it. The broadened definition of news that our young adults adhered to, as well as their news practices, both part of an inherently digital culture, have reinforced the audience's agency in choosing which news to engage in, and calls for a solid understanding of how young audiences construct news relevance in today's multiplex digital media landscape, including which news matters to them and why.

Although we have seen an increased scholarly interest in how news audiences construct news relevance, up until now such studies have only looked at the relevance of traditional news journalism, not paying attention to the widened information repertoires that we, in good company of many other contemporary studies of news perceptions and practices, discuss in this book. In accordance with our phenomenological approach, we understand news relevance from a meaning-making perspective, which means we explore why news matters to young people, and why they care to pay attention to particular information in their daily news feeds, but not others. The heavy, and important, influence of practice theory (cf. Couldry, 2004, 2012) in contemporary audience-centred studies of journalism, has tended to downplay the role of *paying attention to* and *making meaning of* news in contemporary journalism studies. In this chapter we will take a closer look at these dimensions of news relevance and explore how ideas about relevant information play a role in how young people care about news in the digital media landscape.

Approaching the relevance of news

As described in Chapter 2, our 'media day' approach aimed for an open understanding of the young adults' ways of thinking about news, but also a broad understanding of their general information practices – what they valued and found important to be updated and informed about – and if and how news journalism fitted into that picture. This means we did not restrict our discussions to a primarily journalistic perspective of either news or news relevance, and we did not normatively construct news journalism as more relevant than other media content; nor did we specifically ask the young people about how they perceived and practised 'the news' until quite late in the interviews (when this aspect of their media use had often become clear anyway). In these talks, however, *relevance* emerged spontaneously as a core topic of discussion, which basically meant what kind of content the young adults chose to pay attention to in the flow of content on the platforms and other digital media that they used.

Despite an increased interest in news relevance from the audience's point of view, what news relevance is from the audience point of view is still somewhat theoretically unclear. In this chapter we will therefore approach the relevance of news in three main steps. First, we will engage in a phenomenological discussion, exploring news relevance theoretically, building in particular on Berger and Luckmann's (1966) concept of the *structure of relevance*. This discussion concludes in a model of analysis of news relevance from the audience perspective that we have also used when analysing the young adults' discourses about news relevance. We will then move on to analyse through which criteria the young adults choose which news to pay attention to in their everyday lives. This discussion ends up in a matrix of four types of digital news relevance, also contributing to a deeper understanding of the ways digital news was understood to be relevant by our young participants. Lastly, the chapter provides a theoretical definition of news relevance from the audience's perspective. As in the previous chapters, we here work with the distinction between 'news' and 'the news', underscoring how the young adults in the concept of 'news' include everything they consider to be news, in the digital media landscape they inhabit.

News relevance from the audience's perspective

Despite an emerging scholarly interest in how audiences construct news relevance, the number of studies of news relevance from the audience's perspective is still relatively small (see however Martin, 2008; Heikkilä et al., 2010, Heikkilä & Ahva, 2015; Lee & Chyi, 2014; Swart et al., 2017a; Schrøder, 2019). One pioneering study in this field is Pamela Shoemaker and Akiba Cohen's (2006) comparative analysis of how ordinary people evaluated news stories as newsworthy compared with how they were covered by newspapers. In an ambitious comparison of ten countries, they showed generally small, and sometimes even negative, correlations between how newspapers framed news as relevant, compared with how it was evaluated by their audiences, concluding that "there is a disconnection between what ordinary people think is newsworthy and how prominent newspapers display the stories" (p. 110). Another early study is Vivian Martin's (2008) study of *news attendance*, showing how audiences construct news relevance based on assessments of relevance and credibility, on framing, self-identity and orientation affirmation, leading to an 'awareness–relevance–attendance loop' that explains how people acknowledge and pay attention to news they find relevant. Martin particularly highlighted the cultural boundary work involved in the construction of news relevance, relating to aspects of cultural identity, such as gender, race and ideology, something closely related to what we discussed as 'my-topics' in Chapter 4.

Martin's study is particularly relatable for us as it discusses news relevance as something that relates to news content, which is how our participants also framed relevance. From the mid-2010s and onwards, however, studies of news relevance from the audience's perspective have heavily engaged with practice theory (c.f. Couldry, 2004, 2012), leaving the dimension of meaning-making and paying attention to news content somewhat underexplored (see for example Heikkilä & Ahva, 2015; Swart et al., 2017b). In a recent analysis of news users in the UK, however, Kim Christian Schrøder (2019) argued that news relevance is the paramount driver of news consumption and that it is constructed around news that affects people's personal lives (and those who are part of it), and relates to people's earlier experiences, as well as news that users believe the people around them will be interested in, also underlining the shareability of news. Schrøder identified five factors that drive news relevance: 1) news story topic (headline and subheading), 2) brand (preference), 3) proximity (human and geographical), 4) sociability (assumed interest of others) and 5) previous knowledge (from the cross-media environment). Schrøder, similarly to Martin, hence sees news relevance as constructed through audiences' relations to news as content in a social context. We did not ask our participants about what news they found relevant – it was brought up spontaneously by them in our discussions, and we hence did not define relevance for them. The way our participants talked about news relevance, however, had much in common with how news relevance is discussed by Martin (2008) and Schrøder (2019).

It is important to separate journalists' constructions of news relevance from their audiences' when addressing news relevance from an audience perspective, something identified also by other scholars. Besides Martin's *news attendance*, Shoemaker and Cohen (2006) use *newsworthy* to talk about that which media audiences find relevant, while Angela Lee and Add Hsiang Chyi (2014) use *noteworthy* to describe the same thing ('newsworthy' in their terminology is relevance constructed by journalists). Another interlinked concept is *worthwhileness* (Schrøder & Larsen, 2010; Schrøder, 2015), explaining why news users include certain news stories in their daily media repertoire, but not others.

Another interesting take on news relevance from the audiences' perspective which is worth bringing forward here has been developed outside of journalism studies. In a linguistic study of news users' discursive practices, Jena Barchas-Lichtenstein et al. (2021) conducted an analysis of the construction of news relevance as part of daily speech. Building on pragmatist 'relevance theory' (Sperber & Wilson, 1986; Wilson & Sperber, 2006), Barchas-Lichtenstein et al. define relevance as input that makes "a worthwhile difference to the individual's representation of the world" (Wilson & Sperber, 2006, p. 608) and establish relevance as dependent on context, concluding that people's construction of news relevance is related to *the scale of collectivities* to which they subjectively belong. This means that people who feel a belonging to larger-scale collectivities are more likely to find 'the news' relevant than those who feel they belong to smaller-scale collectivities. Based on this, they suggest the following provisional definition of news relevance from the audience's perspective: "a news report is relevant if a news user treats it as impacting the everyday experiences and interactions of either that individual or a larger collectivity of which they describe themselves as a member" (Barchas-Lichtenstein et al., 2021, p. 59). These significant findings also have much in common with Martin's (2008) conclusion that audiences' construction of news relevance include dimensions of identity boundary work.

From previous research of news relevance from the audiences' perspective we know that news relevance is a practice that is framed by the everyday context (Heikkilä et al., 2015; Swart et al., 2017b), and that it is constructed through assessments of topics, framing, brand, credibility and sociability, and related to the identity, experiences, culture and proximity of news to the news audience (Martin, 2008; Schrøder, 2019). We can also note that previous research on news relevance from the audiences' perspective has largely seen news relevance as a coherent concept, that may be explained by different surrounding factors, and that it is affected by the scale of collectivities that people feel they belong to (Barchas-Lichtenstein et al., 2021). Barchas-Lichtenstein et al.'s (2021) provisional definition of news relevance is clarifying and useful, but narrows the notion of news relevance to the scale of collectivities that people feel they belong to, leaving out other important dimensions of news relevance identified by previous research. This leads us to conclude that in order to more fully understand how news relevance is constructed by audiences we need a broader definition of news relevance that can be used as an analytical approach in our investigation. In the following section we will discuss the phenomenological concept of the *structure of relevance* as a way to develop a theoretical understanding of news relevance which may serve as an analytical approach for empirical analysis.

News and the structure of relevance

According to phenomenological theory, the *structure of relevance* transforms the world from chaotic to meaningful by guiding our perceptions and how our interests are shaped, and hence informs where we direct our attention. Husserl called that which competes for our attention in everyday situations *themes* (1999). Everyday life is multidimensional, not least in digital culture where mobile devices multiply the arenas where we can be present and interact with others, forming our culture of information 'abundance' (Boczkowski, 2021). This means several themes simultaneously exist around us, and we constantly have to choose which one(s) to turn our attention to, in our meaning-making practices (Campo, 2015, p. 137). That choice is neither consciously made, nor conducted in a vacuum, but immediate, often unconscious, and socially structured. As developed in the introductory chapter, we think of this practice as an everyday navigation, something we are constantly involved in and routinely practice, but do not pay much attention to, unless something unexpected occurs that breaks our routinised approach in everyday life. The structure of relevance thus helps us not to experience the world as a chaotic arrangement of unique objects, dispersed in space and time, but as *types* we are already familiar with: "mountains", "trees", "fellow-men" or "news" (Schutz, 1953, pp. 7–8). The structure of relevance may hence be understood as a socially derived and conditioned matrix which guides the selective processes defining how we perceive a situation (Campo, 2015, p. 137). It makes us pay attention to the themes in the surrounding world from which we estimate we can construct meaning in the most significant way, given our interests, knowledge, and previous experiences.

As we cannot know everything about reality, Berger and Luckmann (1966, p. 56) mean that we pragmatically "live in a commonsense world of everyday life equipped with specific bodies of knowledge". A person's stock of knowledge is constructed by the sedimentation of our previous experiences, derived from our own experiences or from experiences communicated by others (friends, parents, influencers or 'the news', etc.) (Schutz & Luckmann, 1973, p. 7). The stock of knowledge is a resource that is activated when interpreting and acting, *navigating*, in the world (Campo, 2015, p. 141) and steers our attention to things we believe will be meaningful to us (Berger & Luckmann, 1966, p. 57). An individual's construction of relevance is hence dependent jointly on her *interests*, *previous experiences*, and *social situation* (Berger & Luckman, 1966, p. 59).

Schutz separated three different sets of relevances: 1) thematic or topical relevance (which focuses our attention on themes, and can be both intentional and imposed), 2) interpretive relevance (which assigns meanings to experiences or objects) and 3) motivational relevance (which regulates where we direct our attention). In practice the three types of relevances are interrelated, and Schutz (1970, p. 133) later explained:

> it is quite possible that a shift in the system of interpretational relevances – as with the introduction of a new concept – becomes the starting point for building up a set of new motivational or topical relevances which do not thus far pertain to the familiar stock of knowledge at hand.

This clarification indicates that there are three different *dimensions* built into the structure of relevance, rather than three distinct *kinds* of relevance. Constructing relevance around themes in everyday life thus means we interpret the world around us in relation to earlier experiences and the social situation we are in. When a person for example is confronted with a new topic in the media, she starts to (routinely) interpret and value its relevance according to her position in the world, her previous experiences, and the situation she is currently in. The process of interpretation interplays with the motivation for paying attention to a specific topic and start making meaning, and is hence also intentional. This way of reasoning goes well in line with Martin's (2008) awareness-relevance-attendance loop, where knowledge about specific topics, gained by engaging in the news, breeds relevance and feeds attention for further news on the same topic. Already in the 1970s Schutz pointed out that everyday life contains numerous themes that simultaneously call on our attention, and that various aspects of our identity, experiences, and interests interplay in everyday life. In today's 'abundance' culture, discussions about information overload (Ji et al., 2014; Schmitt et al., 2018) and 'digital disconnection' (Syvertsen & Enli, 2020; Syvertsen, 2020) have shown that this aspect of human life is even more accentuated, underscoring the importance of understanding the construction of news relevance as a kind of navigation, part of our routinely conducted everyday practices (Heikkilä & Ahva, 2015; Swart et al., 2017b; Schrøder, 2019). In the previous chapters we have shown how news today is consumed in various different ways, but often synchronically with other media or other content, intermingled with other everyday practices, or in the interstices of time (Dimmick et al., 2011; Boczkowski et al., 2018), which means it is not given the specific, information-oriented attentiveness we often believe it should, although older media research has shown that people in previous media landscapes also took part of the news in parallel with other everyday tasks (cf. Berelson, 1949; Bausinger, 1984; Morley, 1986; Bengtsson, 2007). Against this backdrop we will here put forward an approach to news relevance from the audience's perspective, built on phenomenological theory, formulated like this:

The construction of news relevance is the process in which an individual decides what news content to pay attention to. News relevance is constructed against the backdrop of earlier experiences, interests, social context, and the everyday situation at hand.

The everyday situation at hand involves both the actual situation – whether one is alone or with others, still or in motion, relating to competing themes in the surrounding world, and so on – and the way the information is mediated (via a certain media technology, another human being, etc.).

Four types of news relevance

It is initially worth again acknowledging that news relevance was not part of any predefined theme that we strived to discuss with our interviewees, but something which appeared spontaneously as the young people were asked to speak freely about what kind of media content and information they considered important to stay updated about, and which they habitually engaged in. Besides the broader discourses about news, journalism and media practices discussed in the previous chapters, the interviews also revolved around the attention the respondents paid to various kinds of media content, and how and why that specific content was considered meaningful to them. As already mentioned, previous research has largely aimed at explaining how the practice of choosing what news to engage in takes place, and why news audiences care to engage in certain topics of news. In this book, we have also looked deeper into the different ways news was considered relevant as it was articulated by our young participants, and from this analysis we have revealed four kinds of news relevance, distinguished from each other by the character and combination of three fundamental dimensions: *purposes, scales* and *temporalities.* In the following, we will first present the four identified types of digital news relevance, and after that discuss the three dimensions that in different combinations constitute news relevance from the young audience's own perspective.

Relevance to know how to act

One core aspect of relevant news that came up in the interviews with the young adults was that news was considered relevant when it provided information that would help our participants (or their close ones) to act adequately and make sound decisions in certain situations, emphasising a strong and familiar connection between news and future action. This aspect of news is closely related to a traditional understanding of news, and this dimension of relevance from the audience's perspective has been identified also by Schrøder (2019). It points to the importance of having access to adequate information to know how to act in diverse situations in everyday life and includes micro as well as macro dimensions of information. Information that one needs to know how to act was often related to very mundane things such as what to wear when leaving home ("Should I wear mittens today?"), how to spend the weekend ("What films does the cinema show?") or where in the world it is safe to spend a future holiday ("What's the political situation in Egypt at the moment?"). It was also seen as relevant to have accurate information in relation to acts of broader civic duties such as how to vote in future elections, although such information was not considered immediately useful in the same way, but as information which could be stored for later occasions. In discussions about news, this aspect of the news-ness of news (Edgerly & Vraga, 2020a, 2020b) relates to the value of being informed about the world, a core dimension of informed citizenship (Moe, 2020). The main purpose of this kind of relevance is *action*, exemplified by one young woman who, in relation to the ongoing pandemic, discussed what kind of information she found relevant to know about like this: "What life is like for us at the moment, what's allowed or not, restrictions, and what is closed down? How to act in everyday life" (Michelle, 19, unemployed, countryside).

Others said they liked to be informed about "general news: what happens in my area, or around me". Such information they found in different channels: in the local newspapers or on TV, but more likely in social media (groups). Penelope, the 19-year-old woman who had finished the gymnasium and currently worked as a childcare assistant while planning to move on to further studies, said she normally paid attention to content and clicked on links in her daily media feed that:

> affect child nurseries around [my city] or would affect public transport in [my city] or if it affects my education. If they, let's say, would remove a course. I don't know exactly, but if it would affect my personal life, or me personally, I would absolutely click on it.
>
> (Penelope, 19, childcare assistant, metropolitan area)

This type of relevance also includes information that is vital for one's close ones: parents, grandparents, relatives, and friends. Abril, a female gymnasium student with an immigrant background from South America, underscored the relevance of news that may be important for her relatives in other parts of the world:

> What's important to me is what happens in the world, but particularly in Spain and Peru, because I have relatives there. So, I want to be informed if there is a protest, or something about [the] Corona [virus] in Spain or Peru. I'm very interested in that. I get my information from Facebook or Instagram, and some of it from Twitter.
>
> (Abril, 18, gymnasium student, metropolitan area)

From a phenomenological perspective this underlines the close relationship between imposed and motivational relevance: it is not enough that information is available in one's media feed, it also needs to fit into one's structure of relevance to be worth paying attention to. Our study was mainly conducted during the Covid-19 pandemic, an unusual period of time when the lives of (young) people across the world were heavily restricted, as schools and universities went online, those who could worked from home, and restaurants, gyms and national borders were closed. Unique for this period however, at least in Sweden, was that these restrictions were constantly shifting due to the spread of the virus and could vary from one week to the next. This unusual situation made updated information about the pandemic immediately relevant for everyone who wanted to act as a responsible human being. The Covid-19 pandemic in this way underlined the critical, even existential, dimension of information, and the urgency of knowing how to act in times of crisis. The pandemic was however not the only example of existentially pressing information put forward by the young adults: Hamza and Yousef, two young male refugees studying to get their gymnasium degree and who lived under the pressure of being thrown out of Sweden if they did not manage to get a stable and secure financial situation within a certain timeframe, underscored the urgency of knowing how to act accurately in their precarious life situation. For them, changed laws regarding permissions to stay in Sweden would determine their future life in a very essential way ("Can I stay in Sweden, or do I have to go back to Afghanistan?"), and they therefore actively tried to minimise the role of 'irrelevant' news that would steal their attention from the kind of information that was most important to them. Hamza said:

> "I basically block pages that publish news of the world. I only follow friends and acquaintances, and they don't normally share news from elsewhere either, so I'm isolated from that kind of news."
>
> (Hamza, 22, gymnasium student, metropolitan area)

Included in this strategy was also that these two young men resisted news from their home country, Afghanistan, as they did not find the information they came across about Afghanistan of importance for knowing how to navigate in their here and now, as refugees in Sweden. In relation to matters that they considered to be of relevance to them, however, they used a broad range of information sources: news journalism, Google search, the Swedish Migration Agency's web page, and so on.

Relevance that keeps one's personal history together

The above discussion confirms what we already know about news relevance from the audience's perspective: that it is personal and relational, relating closely to one's immediate here and now and the actions required to manage everyday life. Another vital way 'news' was considered relevant for the young adults, that made them pay attention to it, was if it related to their earlier life history, what Campo (2015 p. 143) calls "experiences sedimented in my biography". This type of news relevance is relevant for the purpose of keeping one's personal history together and relates to an individual's earlier experiences. This is not only a way of connecting to varied spatio-temporalities of an individual's past, but also strengthens one's own personal chronicle and evokes previous stages in life. Its purpose is *remembering* and it links events in, and information about, the world to one's individual life history. This type of news relevance is constructed specifically (but not only) in relation to two different categories: geographical places where one has previously been, and broader themes relating to one's personal life history (relating to interests one has had, stages in one's individual development, or specific experiences of the past). The importance of geographical proximity for news relevance was identified by Johan Galtung and Marie Holmboe Ruge (1965) in their canonical discussion about news values from a journalistic point of view (see also Schrøder, 2019). Geography, however, also relates to respondents' personal identity and previous experiences beyond proximity, and the spatial dimension of relevance is hence also constructed in relation to places where one, earlier in life, has travelled, met people, experienced things, and made friends. Young Swedes have in general travelled a lot (even though this is of course class-based), and many of the young adults referred to backpacking in Southeast Asia, working their way through Australia, hiking in the US, or different kinds of holidays and school-related trips abroad. Those among our participants who had an immigrant background related to places where they had lived, where their ancestors lived or where they had relatives, and felt a connection to in that way. Such former experiences, including personal connections to people in these places, were described as essential aspects of news relevance. Maria, who worked as a care assistant in a home for the elderly, not only put forward news about the town where her grandparents live as particularly relevant for her to be informed about, she also paid specific attention to what happens in Indonesia:

> Sometimes I check [Covid-19] statistics from Indonesia too. Because I have travelled there with my school, to look at their health care system. We toured around and studied it, how their

health care system worked and other things. And then I got to know new people, and we even became friends.

(Maria, 21, nurse assistant, mid-sized town)

Other themes relating to one's previous life stages, beyond sheer spatiality, were also important in the construction of news relevance. Ylva, a 20-year-old care assistant who lived in a small town, talked openly about her previous struggles to find her way back to normal life after having suffered from bullying in school, developing anorexia and adding several other diagnoses to that. Even though she now had left those problems behind, and saw them as part of her past, she still considered mental (un)health one of the most important topics in the news. She mainly found such information from YouTubers, bloggers and influencers, and Ylva eagerly turned to them for relevant news. In this way, the young people activated varied aspects of their identity and their earlier experiences when constructing news relevance, sometimes consciously articulating it as a strategy to handle the overwhelming flow of information they experienced in their everyday life.

Relevance relating to one's existential sense of self

The *topic* of news is a central aspect of news relevance (see Schrøder, 2019) and as discussed also in previous chapters, the young participants often spontaneously referred to their 'my-topics': one or a few topics that they were so engaged in, that they defined their deepest sense of self. Examples of such topics were feminism, the environment, LGBTQ+ and racism, but also rarer themes were mentioned such as 'the question of cannabis' (relating to broader aspects of individual freedom, censorship and scientific knowledge). Daniel, a 26-year-old hairdresser, put forward his identity as a homosexual as the most defining aspect of his identity when looking for relevant news, going beyond other aspects of his personal life. When asked if he was interested in information about his father's home country, Turkey, he replied:

No, I only know what my dad tells me. And I usually don't listen to that because I don't care too much about it. Unless it would affect *me* in any way. If I would feel "Oh my God, how can they do this or that". But it's just, well ... I don't know, bad things happen everywhere, and you cannot keep up with it all, and engage in it all. You must choose what's ... *your* thing, kind of. (...) I think a lot about what affects me, and that is LGBTQ+ issues. So that's my focus.

(Daniel, 26, hairdresser, metropolitan area)

These 'existential' topics were framed as unique interests, with a special position in the young person's idea of who they were. Despite being generally well informed in the areas of the 'my-topics', the young adults wanted to know *everything* about these topics and kept updated via various sources of information: influencers, YouTube channels, podcasts, activist accounts, memes, friends with specific knowledge in the area, but also news journalism locally, nationally and globally. Interest in such topics was framed as temporally and geographically indifferent; it was not important where in the world an event had occurred or what place the news referred to; as Daniel expressed it: "if they change a law in Uganda that's harmful to LGBTQ+ people, I want to know!" News relating to such topics was deeply connected to the young adults' identity, and this kind of news was considered relevant – besides its topical relevance – as it contributed to deepening their existential sense of self.

Relevance for situating oneself in the world

The last identified theme is that of relevance to a broader understanding of the world, a theme which is not explicitly useful in relation to any identified situation, but that gives a broader orientation to the world and puts it in perspective. If the purpose of the former category was to deepen one's individual sense of self, the purpose of this type of news is rather to provide a broader understanding of the world and of one's own position in it. This dimension of news relevance, just as the already discussed 'my-topics' embraced the young person's interest in the broader structures that frame singular events, structures what they could also relate to their own position in the world (relating to what Clark & Marchi (2017) call 'inserting oneself in the story'; see also Martin, 2008; Schrøder, 2019). This purpose is less centripetal than the above-discussed types of relevance, and more directed to the lives and conditions of unknown others and one's own relation to them. In the discussions with the young adults, this type of relevance was articulated in statements such as "it is important to be informed, to have a broad general education" (c.f. *bildung*), and "it is important to have knowledge, not only about your own world, but also about other people's lives". As such, it also relates more directly to the public dimension of news, and to *public connection* (Couldry et al., 2007a; Kaun, 2012; Moe & Ytre-Arne, 2022), as discussed in Chapter 1.

This kind of relevance was related both to specific events, for example political elections in foreign countries, or natural disasters, such as flooded areas on the other side of the world, but also to larger societal structures, such as economics, racism, or climate change. Such news was brought forward by several of the interviewees as it engaged them to the extent that they started to reconsider their own identity and their own position in the world from a global perspective. One example that was going on in parallel with our fieldwork, and that was brought up in many interviews, was the Black Lives Matter movement and the killing of the African-American George Floyd. This event and its aftermath were greatly covered by news journalism, but the young adults in general engaged more with, and were more deeply moved by what they learnt about this affair in social media. Many described how their social media feeds were flooded with BLM-related content during this period, and how they 'dived into' social media to search for, and share, information about it. The killing of George Floyd and all the things that happened after it not only dominated their social media feeds in terms of number of posts. Several of our participants also talked about how they were deeply emotionally moved by what happened and started to question and rethink their own position in the world, as white, privileged Swedes in a peaceful Nordic country. This also sparked them to act and show solidarity in different ways and through different channels. Axel, a 23-year-old man who studied music production, described such an existential awakening and willingness to actually do something, coming from what he learnt from his Instagram feed and some music-oriented pages on Facebook.

> It was everywhere, more or less. I mean, my entire Instagram was filled with just black pictures, so the entire feed was just black. And I posted about it too, because it's so important to pay attention to it, actually. To *do* something about it, if you can. On Facebook, you can take part of what they call 'events': you can see people who shows black culture and black art. So, they show you black musicians and artists. And it's been *so* nice to follow, I think. And it is *so* important to follow and support, and help, sort of, as much as you can.
>
> (Axel, university student, 23, mid-sized town)

Others shared similar stories about global injustice disclosed in social media; police brutality in Nigeria, democratic backsliding, feminist activism across the world, LGBTQ+-related issues in different countries, and so on, and how that made them rethink their own situation as human beings and their (privileged) position in the world, from a global perspective. Such globally spread world events, that the young adults felt were often superficially (if at all) covered by 'the news', were important when negotiating what kind of human being they were, and wanted to become. The young adults in this sense also considered 'news' they received from social media more meaningful than 'the news' as it related to the structural dimension and broader consequences of news events, rather than just to single events (something which will be developed more in depth in the next chapter). Another aspect that was brought forward in this discussion is also the broader spectrum of means of communication available in social media 'news', compared with 'the news', for example music, visual material and memes, that was seen as something that made 'news' in social media more meaningful than news journalism, as it made it easier to *feel* the news. Such broadening and affective dimensions of world events that, according to the young adults, were often superficially (if at all) covered by news journalism, were important for the young adults, for their understanding of the broader structures of the world, and for negotiating their own role in it.

This broader understanding of the world and negotiation of one's own position in it was sometimes also related to more specified geographical and socio-spatial communities. Jennifer, a 23-year-old woman who was studying to become a singer, considered Instagram the perfect news provider as it kept her up to date with her specific 'my-topics' (feminism was one of them) as well as information relevant to the different communities to which she belonged. When asked what media she first checked when she woke up in the morning, she said:

> It's absolutely Instagram, yes (...) I check what people do. I forgot to tell you that I follow quite a few feminist accounts where I get news, and the 'search bubble' also shows some news and stuff. I get so much information on Instagram about the world, about my friends and what other people find important.
>
> (Jennifer, 23, student, metropolitan area)

This type of news relevance relates well to what Barchas-Lichtenstein et al. (2021) discuss as the link between the collectivities that people belong to, and the kind of news they find relevant. It is closely related to one's stock of knowledge, guided by one's interest in the world, and one's own position in it.

Purposes, scales and temporalities of news relevance

The above-presented analysis has resulted in four ideal types of news relevance, constituted by variations of three dimensions: 1) *purposes*, which describe the different ways news was thought to be meaningful in the everyday life of the young adults; 2) *temporalities*, which distinguish between temporal directions inherent in the ways the themes become meaningful for their audiences, and 3) *scales*, which point to what Barchas-Lichtenstein et al. (2021) underline as the scale of the collectivities to which people subjectively belong. The four kinds of news relevance, and the three dimensions that constitute them, can be presented as a matrix of types of news relevance, and in the following we will discuss the three dimensions of news relevance from the audiences' perspective that make up the model.

Table 1: Four types of 'news' relevance.

Types of 'news' relevance	Purpose	Temporality	Scale
Relevance to know how to act	Acting	Prospective (Future)	Me/known others
Relevance that keeps one's personal history together	Remembering	Retrospective (Past)	Me/known others
Relevance relating to one's existential sense of self	Existing	Introspective (Present)	Me
Relevance for situating oneself in the world	Understanding	Prospective (Future)	Unknown others

Research about audiences' news relevance has often emphasised relevance that interrupts our expectations and makes us aware of something *new* as the most significant kind of relevance (Schrøder, 2019; c.f. Schutz & Luckmann, 1973, p. 189). Yet, we also know that people find news relevant if it, in addition to this, relates to their spatial belonging, earlier experiences and cultural identity (Martin, 2008; Schrøder, 2019), something which resonates well with how our participants constructed news relevance. Besides a largely different approach, there are also obvious empirical connections to Berelsons (1949) old study of what makes news- reading meaningful to its audiences. In this respect, the presented analysis of news relevance in digital culture confirms what we already know from previous research. The young adults that we talked to considered news relevant to pay attention to if it was likely to be useful in a nearer, or more remote, future for themselves, or for identified people in their social circles. In this way, it fits well with Shibutani's notion of news as "information that is important to someone" (1966, p. 40), although our analysis also showed that news relevance is broader and more diverse than this. Besides information to act upon, news is also considered relevant by the young adults in relation to remembrance, existence and to situate themselves in the world. This means the thematic aspects of news relevance, when understood from a perspective of attention and meaning-making, are more complex and multifaceted than previous research has acknowledged.

The second dimension that the analysis disclosed is the variation in temporalities of news relevance in digital culture. As mentioned previously, news is often thought of as that which provides us with applicable information needed to orient in the world and to make pertinent decisions in everyday life. This means news has impending relevance and steers our attention to yet unknown demands of the future. Orientation towards the future is however not the only temporality innate in the identified types of digital news relevance, relating to the different 'zones of intermediacy' of news experiences discussed by Keightley and Downey (2018). An orientation to the future is obvious in the first type of news relevance, information we need to know how to act, as well as, although more loosely, in the last category, information to situate oneself in the world. A future orientation is inherent in different social and existential aspects of being and *becoming*, but the young adults also constructed relevance in relation to themes that connect them with their own personal history, as a way of keeping their own self, and its social networks, together, as well as around topics ('my-topics') that they relate closely to who they are and want to be, from a more existential point of view. The different kinds of news relevance constructed by the young people hence hold both retrospective and introspective directions, enlarging the temporal dimension of news beyond its futurity.

The attention- and meaning-oriented perspective on news relevance in digital culture employed here also involves the dimension of scale. The scale of news relevance has to do with to whom, or what, information is deemed meaningful. From a phenomenological point of view, we can make a distinction between the way news in digital culture relates to consociates (those we meet face to face, or have a personal relation to) and contemporaries (of whom we have only less detailed recollections, or know merely by hearsay), a distinction described as a continuum of degrees of anonymity (Berger & Luckmann, 1966, pp. 46, 47; also Schutz, 1967). Barchas-Lichtenstein et al.'s (2021) linguistic analysis of how audiences construct relevance in relation to news journalism suggests that news is considered relevant to a higher extent by those who feel a subjective belonging to larger-scale collectivities compared with those who subjectively belong to smaller-scaled collectivities. We can conclude that three of the four identified types of news relevance relate to consociates, and only one to contemporaries. And even though the last type of news relevance – relevance for situating oneself in the world – had a broader orientation to the public world, and to public connection, the *relevance* of such news was constructed in relation to one's own position in the world.

Conclusion

The above analysis of news relevance has shown how news matters in complex ways: besides future action, also for remembering one's history and the people that are part of it, defining one's own identity and positioning oneself in the world. It should, however, also be underlined that even though one of the four identified types of news relevance relates to the lives of unknown others, the remaining three types of news relevance construct news in digital culture as relevant from a perspective mainly relating to one's consociates, one's own personal *networks*. Such aspects of news relevance are also underlined by the possibility for media users, in digital culture, to curate their own news repertoire in order to fit well with their individual structure of relevance. Often implicit in discussions about news is its purpose of keeping citizens informed, so that they can make sound judgements in relation to voting and other civic duties (Schudson, 1998). A basic requirement of news, seen from this perspective, is that it is new, and provides new information about certain topics to its audiences. From a phenomenological perspective, this means the purpose of news is to introduce us to *themes* that add to our current knowledge, and that we will deem worthwhile paying attention to. In this chapter we have, however, in line with other contemporary news audience research, problematised this point of view and shown that although news may be considered relevant by audiences because it is new, the relevance of news is more multifaceted regarding both its purposes, temporalities and scales than we previously believed – and its newness is often, but not always, emphasised from an individual and relational perspective, rather than from the perspective of a joint public sphere. This underscores that our participants want news to be useful or relatable, either for them, or for the people they have relations with. Based on both the theoretical discussion and the empirical analysis, we can hence formulate a definition of news relevance from the audience's perspective:

> The construction of news relevance is the process in which an individual decides what news content to pay attention to. News relevance is constructed against the backdrop of social context and connections, earlier experiences, interests, and the everyday situation at hand. News relevance varies in terms of purposes, scales and temporalities.

It is important to, again, underline that the process of deciding what mediated information to pay attention to, part of the *navigation of news*, is a routinised everyday practice and hence not (always) conscious or voiced, even for the individual involved in it. Following from the theoretical definition of news relevance suggested here, built around the practice of *paying attention* to a piece of information in a specific everyday situation and a social context, and the *meaning-making* processes around it, we can conclude that both the young adults' constructions of 'news' and of relevance are more *centripetal* and oriented to their *relational networks* and the consociates that construct them, compared with the idea about news as that which connects people to the public sphere (even though elements of the public and public connection are included in it). From a theoretical point of view, this clearly underlines that the structure of relevance is both *individual* and *relational* as it is created in relation to the individual's *interaction with the world*. This is in line with Schutz's explanation that the private situation of an individual "is always a situation within the group, his private interests are interests with reference to those of the group (whether by way of particularization or antagonism), his private problems are necessarily in a context with the group's problems" (Schutz, 1955, p. 238, quoted in Campo, 2015, p. 145).

This finding resonates well with contemporary news research, that has found similar notions of personal meaning-making in relation to news, and of 'inserting oneself into the story' (Clark & Marchi, 2017 also Barchas-Lichtenstein et al., 2021, p. 59; Schrøder, 2019; Martin, 2008). These dimensions of news relevance may at first glance seem to indicate that young audiences are primarily interested in themes relating to themselves and the people they already know. Yet, rather than pointing to an increased individualisation, it underscores the relationality of the self, and the importance of one's networks and personal relationships when constructing the world and what is relevant in it. One of the types of news relevance identified here, *relevance for situating oneself in the world*, also includes broader interests and concerns about things that do not immediately relate to one's own situation and everyday life, but that help in understanding how one's own position in the world makes sense in relation to (unknown) others. The above speaks against the interpretation that young people form a highly individualised generation and only care about themselves. But if news relevance, as suggested here, is 'the process in which an individual decides what news content to pay attention to' and which 'is constructed against the backdrop of an individual's social context and connections, earlier experiences, interests, and the everyday situation at hand', the distribution of news in digital, and particularly social, media, where fragments of information come from varied sources in a stream of mixed content, and where people independently, and according to their own interests, can construct their own personal news feed, may point to an idea of *the public*, which has more in common with John Dewey's (1916/1923) notion than with the Habermasian idea of the public sphere (and public connection). According to this perspective a public is constructed of a group of people "who regard themselves as likely to become involved in the consequences of an event and are sufficiently concerned to interest themselves in the possibility of control" (Shibutani, 1966, p. 38). A public, according to Dewey, is identified by its common focus of attention, which means it is characterised by a conversation around a certain issue or problem and as such forms "a mostly unruly, non-organised and ephemeral phenomenon that comes together around a particular topic" (Ojala & Ripatti-Torniainen, 2023, p. 153). Such sociological perspective on publics has a stronger focus on the audience's own agency in forming a public and hence holds potential to meet the criticism often directed towards a Habermasian notion of the public sphere and, particularly, the role of news journalism in it. Seeing news audiences as forming narrower and more ephemeral publics in this way fits well with the way the young adults talked about news relevance and how news must be relatable, meaningful, and useful from either their own individual perspective, or that of the people in their networks.

Chapter 6
News as facts and stories

In this book, our discussions about young people's information practices have often revolved around media use *beyond* news journalism, as few – although some – of our respondents considered news journalism the most essential information provider in their everyday life (however, as we have discussed in the previous chapters, most of them considered news journalism a reliable and trustworthy source of information).

This chapter, on the other hand, will be dedicated to a closer look at perceptions about news journalism and the meaning-making around it, or, more correctly put, to a closer look at why the young adults, just as youth across the world, often preferred other information formats to 'the news' when constructing their 'media day'. From previous research we have learnt that 'news avoiders' – people who regularly consume little news – avoid news first because of the overload of news, but also due to the negative content in news, as well as the technological features of aggressive algorithmic news technology. Digital media have multiplied the total volume of news available in the world, and this abundance of information paralyses people, and hinders them from engaging in meaningful news practices rather than helping them to find the information they would find worthwhile. As Tali Aharoni et al. (2021) have suggested though, digital media have not only transformed the amount of news and information in the world, but also how that information is produced, distributed, perceived and practised. Here, we propose the idea that news journalism, distributed and practised via digital, mainly social, media, is perceived mainly as *facts* and as such is regarded as irrelevant, meaningless, and boring (for a similar discussion see Hendrickx, 2024). To find meaningful and valuable information, the young adults we interviewed instead turned to other media formats, particularly in social media. This suggestion, again has similarities with the findings that Clark and Marchi presented in *Young People and the Future of News* (2017), where they put forward the dullness of news journalism and the problems with journalistic storytelling, articulated by teens participating in their study, as the main reasons why young people refuse to engage in a majority of news journalism. Our suggestion is similar, yet different, as we here present an alternative perspective on what a meaningful story is, and what makes its value lasting.

Use and non-use of news

Before moving into the empirical analysis, we will here briefly discuss the practice of side-stepping 'the news' in search of vital information. This practice is in contemporary news research sometimes conceptualised as *intentional news avoidance*, something which has been given substantial attention by academics and news organisations during the last decades (Park, 2019; Karlsen et al., 2020; Goyanes et al., 2023; Andersen et al., 2024). News avoidance is also often seen as a primarily passive behaviour, conducted by those who lack political engagement, have a weak feeling for their citizen duties, or less established routines for consuming news. Based on her studies of politically engaged, but alternative, audiences, Jennifer Rauch (2020) however, argues that resisting the news can be a deliberate political statement, part of a critique of the perspectives and voices of mainstream media (see also Clark & Marchi, 2017).

Despite voices like Rauch's and Clark's and Marchi's, trying to understand more deeply young people's own reasons for sidestepping 'the news', the concept of news avoidance is often normative and therefore risks missing the nuances of people's media practices, as has been pointed out by Mikko Villi et al. (2022). They suggest we make a conceptual distinction between those who actively avoid news journalism (as part of an alternative information practice) and those who simply do not use it and conceptualise the latter practices as 'non-use'. From our fieldwork, conducted among a wide range of ordinary young adults, of which only a small minority were heavily engaged in political activism, this conceptualisation provides a more adequate articulation of what many non-journalism practices are about, as 'news avoidance', along with many other kinds of (non) media practices – for example sports avoidance, porn avoidance or podcast avoidance – may not be such a strong statement as the word 'avoidance' assumes. As we will show here, many of the young people we talked to did not articulate their non-use of 'the news' as such a strongly distinguishing practice, but resulting from the fact that news journalism was neither considered the only, nor the most relevant, important, or meaningful, media content to keeping them updated about what is relevant in their world. The idea of non-use of news journalism as an illegitimate everyday practice is connected to the idea of the central role of news journalism in democracy and keeping up with the news as a citizen duty. But if young people today (in line with the findings of, for example, Peters et al., 2022 and Stald, 2023), keep up to date about the world through a broad palette of information including channels far beyond 'the news', and hence in their everyday lives habitually sidestep news journalism but not relevant information about the world as *they* see it, why is it so? Clark and Marchi, in their study of the connective news practices of teenagers (2017), point to the problem of journalistic narration as one of

the factors explaining young people's disillusionment with 'the news', in combination with the streamlined implicit audience of news journalism, and its business
models, leading to a loss of authority of journalism. Our open discussions with
the young people, where we did not ask them specifically about their use of
news journalism, also often revolved around how dull the young people considered 'the news' to be, and how they turned to other media formats to find meaning
and content that spoke *to them* and *with them*, when searching for information
they found valuable in relation to their own lives and those that are part of it.

Sometimes when people's non-use of news journalism is discussed it is framed
as a problem and as something different from how equivalent practices were constituted half a century ago, although our argument in Chapter 4 contributes to a
questioning of this. Here, we will seek an alternative understanding of why
many young adults today disregard news journalism in their daily media routines
and point to some old and new explanations of how and why they understand, talk
about and practise (or not) 'the news' the way they do. Just as Clark and Marchi
(2017), we see *storytelling* as a key dimension in understanding these news practices, although in this book the practices of not using 'the news' have more the
character of non-use of news journalism, rather than a deliberately alternative
practice (although we also found elements of that among our participants). Therefore, the notion of what constitutes a story is in this context discussed somewhat
differently from what Clark and Marchi do. Phenomenologically, we will look at
the non-use of news journalism through the lens of the 'horizon' of a theme,
where a theme, as we discussed in Chapter 4, is that which competes for our attention in everyday life, in light of a theoretical perspective on news as events, facts
and storytelling, borrowed from journalism scholar Tuchman (1976) and cultural
theorist Walter Benjamin (1936/2006). Tuchman and Benjamin have both, in related but different ways, discussed the significance of storytelling in our understanding of the emerging information society, and the role of news in it. Their different
perspectives will be used to dig deeper into, and shed light on, the logic of contemporary 'non-use' of news journalism, and hence to contribute to a deeper understanding of why young audiences are 'abandoning' news journalism today.

News journalism as stories and events

Today everyone knows that news is a social construction. Framing theory is a
hugely used perspective in contemporary journalism studies (Entman, 1993,
2007), originally building on the works of Tuchman (1978), Herbert Gans (1979)
and Todd Gitlin (1977), who explored and developed the constructivist perspective
on news. Tuchman, as mentioned in the introductory chapter, introduced the 'win-

dow metaphor' as a way to understand how news journalism opened people's views to the world, while simultaneously creating the limitations to, or frames of, what was actually possible to see. Another of Tuchman's important contribution to contemporary journalism theory is her claims about news as stories, and of journalists as storytellers. In the short article "Telling Stories" (1976), Tuchman argued that "reports of news are *stories* – no more, but no less" (p. 93), also emphasising that storytelling is a craft, a practice, that transforms an *event*, consisting of sheer facts, to a *story* that is meaningful to those who listen to it. Drawing from Erwing Goffman's (1975, pp. 10–11) notion of 'frame analysis', she distinguished between the raw *events*, that she discussed as originally being "strips of the everyday world" or "an arbitrary slice or cut from the stream of on-going activity", and the *frame*, which is "the principle of organisation that governs events – at least social ones – and our subjective involvement in them" (Tuchman, 1976, p. 94).

In this short but important text, Tuchman sets out the argument that news journalism provides the frame that transforms strips of social reality into meaningful stories. "As frames", she said, "news stories offer definitions of social reality" (1976, p. 94). One of her arguments for this, building on her extensive ethnographical newsroom studies, was that when news reporters talked in their own words about their journalistic work, these discourses revolved around the making of stories, rather than reporting about events (1976, pp. 95; 1978). Claiming that news is stories may imply that it is neither factual nor objective, something which may be controversial to say, but Tuchman argued that "being a reporter who deals in facts and being a storyteller who produces tales are not antithetical activities" (Tuchman, 1976, p. 96).

In our contemporary society, public discourse about news journalism has largely changed, and the claims that Tuchman made in the 1970s are common knowledge today. It is no longer suspicious to talk openly about 'the angle' of an article, and journalists often directly state what kind of quote they want an interviewee to deliver before starting the interview. The idea of news being stories has in the light of the decreasing interest in news among audiences worldwide, and particularly so when looking at younger audiences, also resulted in a heightened discussion about the lack of narration in news journalism, where an increasing emphasis on the narrative dimension of news journalism is sometimes put forward as a solution to the problem with audiences who turn away from news journalism (Clark & Marchi, 2017; Buozis & Creech, 2018).

In light of these discussions, it is important that we reflect not only on the role of storytelling in news journalism, but also on what a good story is. What makes a good (news) story from the audience's point of view? What characteristics, features and values constitute it? Popular culture research told us long ago that storytelling involves more than a narrative structure, as it comprises the content of the story, the way it is practised and the situated context of this practice, in combination with the worldview and meaning-making of those who take part in the story (cf. Radway, 1984/2009). In his much-cited, but also controversial, *The Uses of Enchantment: The Meaning and Importance of Fairy Tales* (1976/2010), psychoanalyst and cultural theorist Bruno Bettelheim argued that fairy tales help children to handle important existential problems such as separation anxiety, oedipal conflict and sibling rivalries, and that the intense violence and threatening emotions involved in many fairy tales serve to bring forward and shed light on what may well be going on in the child's mind anyway. This implies that stories are both existential and anchored in the reader's own everyday struggles and dilemmas, and emphasises the connection between a story and the audience's own everyday situation. This dimension of storytelling has also been discussed by Frankfurt school scholar Walter Benjamin, as he, just as Tuchman later did, discussed the relation between stories and facts in information society, hence also problematising the surrounding societal (and technological) context of storytelling. In his essay "The Storyteller" (1936/2006), built mainly on an analysis of Russian 19th century novelist Nikolai Leskov, Benjamin put forward three dimensions that are fundamental in all stories. First, he said, stories are *important.* This does not mean important in the same way as news is important – for society at large – but rather that they are important from the individual's own point of view, essential for him/her, and in that sense useful. Secondly, Benjamin said that stories are *enduring*, which points to them as meaningful beyond the immediate here and now. Thirdly, Benjamin claimed, stories involve a *sharing of experiences.* The first and second dimensions point to the timeless dimension of stories, which means that (traditional) storytelling holds lasting values, and does not aim to convey the pure essence of the thing, like information or a report has to (Benjamin, 1936/2006, p. 367). The third dimension, storytelling as a shared experience, refers both to the very situation where stories are told to a group (such as around a fireplace), or to the established relationship between a specific storyteller and the person who listens to (or reads) him/her. Nicolai Leskov is, according to Benjamin, a rare example among modern novelists, as he manages to establish such a bond with his readers, even in the detached kind of storytelling that the 19th century novel provides. In his reasoning about the essential characteristics of stories (and storytelling), Benjamin also emphasises the *craftmanship* embedded in storytelling as an artisan form of communication.

As part of the argument about the essence of stories and storytelling, Benjamin furthermore presents an analysis of the characteristics of information and the emerging information society, and in this venture he also touches upon news journalism, that he sees as the epic form of communication signifying the information society. Benjamin points to some of the core features of information that he believes make it less meaningful than traditional stories. Information, he says, is first ephemeral, and therefore "does not survive the moment when it was new" (1936/2006, p. 366). Secondly, he also claims that information is too closely related to facts, as it "lays claim to prompt verifiability" (1936/2006, p. 365). While he argues that the essence of storytelling is closely anchored in basic dimensions of human life, such as history, memory, morality and the 'meaning of life', information, on the other hand, is rapid, facts-based (verifiable) and geographically dispersed. Information, and in contemporary society thus also news journalism, hence provides people with truthful facts but falls short when it comes to bringing meaning and a lasting value to their lives. He says that "every morning brings us the news of the globe, and yet we are poor in noteworthy stories" (Benjamin, 1936/2006, p. 365). It may be clear by now that Benjamin mourns the decline of storytelling in the emerging information society, and the rise of new epic forms of communication, such as news journalism and information, which have come to take its place. He specifically notes the symbiotic relationship between the press and information, and how the capitalist information society has engaged the middle classes as its warriors. He also warns of the consequences of this:

> We recognise that with the full control of the middle class, which has the press as one of its most important instruments in fully developed capitalism, there emerges a form of communication which, no matter how far back its origin may lie, never before influenced the epic form in a decisive way. (...) [T]his new form of communication is information.
>
> (Benjamin, 1936/2006, p. 365)

In the new epic form of communication in information society, Benjamin saw how traditional kinds of storytelling "receded into the archaic" (1936/2006, p. 365) and how new emerging forms of communication (i. e., news and information) slowly replaced them as the most significant kind of communication. This process, he says, obstructs meaningful storytelling in contemporary society, something which risks transforming society as a whole, if we are to again acknowledge Dewey's notion that society exists in communication (1916/1923). A traditional storyteller has a similar role as a teacher or a sage: he offers help, not in one situation, but *for the whole life*, while information promises quick, updated facts, which also convey the assurance of perpetual novelty.

Built into Benjamin's argument is also a critique of the working conditions in which news journalism is created. The creation of meaningful stories lies in the hearty craftmanship of the storyteller, he argues, which he said that the emergent forms of communication work in information society destroyed. Benjamin put forward his argument about the craftmanship of journalists in the 1930s, and today we have an even more heightened debate about under which conditions meaningful news is created and distributed (Westlund & Lewis, 2014; Vulpius, 2023), not least in the light of AI and other digital technologies.

When we put these two intellectuals, Tuchman and Benjamin, side by side, we find two contradictory ways of theorising news journalism, but in which the relation between facts (as information about events) and stories is essential to both. Benjamin argues that journalism and storytelling are contradictory phenomena, as storytelling is "inclined to borrow from the miraculous", while information (and hence news journalism) is required to present accurate facts and as such is incompatible with the spirit of storytelling (1936/2006, p. 365). But whereas Benjamin saw storytelling as an epistemic opposition to news journalism, Tuchman believed that journalism is simultaneously events *and* stories, which as two sides of the same coin – meaning and information, subjective and objective – are equally important dimensions of news, and not at all divergent. Yet, even though these two thinkers have contradictory beliefs regarding the relation between information and storytelling and the role of news in this, they do agree that storytelling in news journalism does not (only) relate to its narrative dimensions – such as the tale, plot or storyline – but also to the deeper and more fundamental dimensions of human life and culture. Benjamin puts this argument forward when claiming that "The storyteller is the figure in which the righteous man encounters himself" (Benjamin, 1936/2006, p. 378) while Tuchman says that the framing of news as stories "lay[s] a world before us" (Tuchman, 1976, p. 97). In the following section we will move on to see how the young adults related to news journalism, as facts and storytelling.

News journalism as facts and events

The first distinction that Benjamin, just as Tuchman, makes between stories and information, or events, is that stories are meaningful while events are 'strips of reality', without deeper meaning. This distinction came up spontaneously when talking about media use and the meaning of news with the young adults. As we have seen in the previous chapters, our participants, just as most other young people in Sweden and the (Western) world, used social media continuously throughout the day and often put forward social media as their prime source of news and information. We also know from previous research that social media today is the main provider of news journalism for young people, in Sweden as well as in many other countries in the world.[1] This means that young people in large parts of the world meet news journalism mainly in the shape it takes in social media. Some of the young adults followed social media services of newspapers and public service broadcasting, and hence came across and/or took part in the headlines of the news that these news providers published. Others did not use social media particularly (or at all) for information-seeking purposes, but still received news from news organisations in social media, as people in their networks shared it.

As already mentioned in Chapter 2, we kept our interviews open and did not specifically ask our respondents about news journalism until late in the interviews (if they did not, spontaneously, start to talk about it when telling us about their daily media use and information practices). With those who did not talk about, or just marginally mentioned, news journalism, we late in the interviews asked them about it, in terms such as 'We have not talked about news (journalism)…?' Some respondents directly said "no", stating that news journalism was not of any particular interest to them, and that they did not use it in everyday life. Some said they sometimes came across 'the news' in social media, yet others had friends and family who shared certain news articles or TV news with them in varied media channels as well as face to face (cf. Peters et al., 2022). When asked to elaborate a bit more on news journalism: what it was and what it meant to them, the core value of news journalism that was brought up concerned news as facts and objective information, something Clark and Marchi (2017) in their study of US teenagers also came across. Facts is a cultural phenomenon which is generally highly praised in contemporary society, as well as in contemporary educational discourses (in Sweden as well as elsewhere), and the societal discourse about news journalism as consisting of *facts* may have affected how this discussion turned out in the interviews. Despite this, the role of facts and information saturated these discussions, exemplified by a male waiter (Johannes, 26, waiter, university town) who emphasised that news "really needs to be based on facts, that's essential!" News journalism was by others said to be "relevant facts" and "an event that affects a larger group of people". One young man added that "I think that if you are to define news, it's quite important that people get information about facts, that are shared with others" (Axel, 23, university student, mid-size town). Another male university student underlined the objective dimension of news and said that:

---

1 https://svenskarnaochinternet.se/rapporter/svenskarna-och-internet-2021/medietjanster-och-ny hetskonsumtion/.

> There has to be news that is genuinely straight forward, just straight ahead, no angles. That's
> what we should protect the most, that you must be able to take part of world news, and to see
> and understand things without being influenced politically.
>
> (Edward, 21, university student, university town)

Others did not explicitly mention facts when talking about news journalism, yet underlined the objective dimension of news when describing its character. Absalom, an 18-year-old gymnasium student, living in a lower-middle-class suburb in a metropolitan area, said that:

> News is news, it's things that happen. Important and unimportant things. Things that happen
> in the world of football is also news, but maybe not as important as if it happens in politics, or
> the world. Things that happen, that's news.
>
> (Absalom, 18, gymnasium student, metropolitan area)

In the same group discussion, another young man added: "[news] is things that happen, that are shared and that we may be interested in. It wants to distribute information" (Simon, 18, gymnasium student, metropolitan area).

Others revealed how they approached 'the news' selectively to only get the facts, as news was seen as so politicised that they tried "to cut [politics] out and just look at the facts" (Erik, 23, student, university town). Facts and information were in general put forward as the main reason why news is considered valuable, and the main reason to include news in one's daily information repertoire. At the same time, facts were neither considered essential in the young people's own information practices, nor considered particularly interesting, as the facts provided by 'the news' seldom made any substantial difference in their own lives. This way of reasoning was exemplified by an 18-year-old man who lived in an underprivileged suburb in a metropolitan area, who told a story about when he was misled by a false piece of news about the death of North Korean leader Kim Jong-un. The young man regretted being fooled by the piece of 'fake news', but at the same time did not make a big deal of it, as he did not see that information as particularly important anyway. Kim Jong-un was, according to the incorrect piece of news, supposed to have died during an operation, something which later turned out to be wrong. When reflecting on the occasion, the young man said: "I shouldn't have believed in it. I don't remember if I believed in it, I honestly don't really think I cared. I don't think I had an opinion about it" (Simon, 18, gymnasium student, metropolitan area).

This quote conveys the distinction between facts and opinion, revealing a hierarchy that was commonly brought up by the young adults, where an opinion, either their own individual opinion or one that was shared by someone else, about the facts provided by 'the news' defined whether the piece of news was worthwhile (Schrøder, 2015) bothering about or not. Interesting enough to engage in, the young adults meant, was news that they cared about, that made a serious difference to them, in their lives, as human beings, while other pieces of news were not seen as particularly essential to be informed about after all. This distinction between facts and opinions makes a good illustration of the distinction between news as facts about *events* – things that have happened – and news as *stories* that bring meaning to people's lives.

The futility of 'the news'

Another of the essential dimensions of storytelling put forward by Benjamin in his analysis of the distinction between stories and information, is that stories provide an enduring value. This is what makes a story truly 'useful', a usefulness built into the essential qualities it brings to the lives of its audiences, such as "a moral", "some practical advice" or "a proverb or maxim". Benjamin put forward that the storyteller "has counsel for his readers" while also pointing out that if "having counsel" sounds a bit old-fashioned it is because the communicability of experience is decreasing in modern society (Benjamin, 1936/2006, p. 364). The epic form of communication in information society – news journalism – emphasises, Benjamin meant, a loss of communicative meaning as news provides neither important moral guidance, useful advice nor lasting axioms to live by.

This distinction between news as events and stories was also brought up in the interviews in discussions about the 'futility' of 'the news'. Although our respondents, as has also been found in other studies (i.e., Casero-Ripollés, 2012), acknowledged news journalism mainly as trustworthy and legitimate communication, they also considered it boring (see Clark & Marchi, 2017; Hendrickx, 2024). This idea, that news journalism is 'good' but boring, was for example expressed in a discussion about 'the news' by a group of middle-class female friends, where one of them stated that "you know that the information you get [from 'the news'] is correct" but yet "it's really boring. Really long texts, no Insta stories, just some small pictures. I mean, influencers are more fun, in that sense" (Kajsa, 21, student, metropolitan area). Elias, an unemployed man who adhered to a very outspoken 'news finds me' perception (De Zúñiga et al., 2017; De Zúñiga et al., 2020), and hence did not actively search for any kinds of news in his everyday media practices, still said that 'the news' was his prime source of information, at the same time as he was "tired of reading about all the shit that happens all the time. I really don't care about many of the bad things [in 'the news']" (Elias, 23, unemployed, metropolitan area).

News journalism, in general considered a legitimate but mainly facts-based and somewhat boring, kind of information, was by the young adults often seen as lacking meaning and hence neither particularly important, nor interesting. Such an approach to news was articulated by a young man who said that although he considered 'the news' to be valuable information, he did not appreciate all the (useless) micro-details it flooded him in, exemplifying with details from statistics about the real estate market:

> I don't think I need to know that it has gone down "more than 23%". Or *of course* that can be good to know. But it's not really relevant to store in your head, when it comes to facts.
>
> (Axel, 23, university student, mid-sized town)

This way of seeing news as mainly consisting of micro-facts, a bit boring and rather meaningless, can be understood through the phenomenological concept of horizon, and how the horizon of every theme that catches our attention in everyday life shapes how it is made meaningful to us (Schutz & Luckmann, 1973). If we see news as themes that we meet in everyday life, and that compete for our attention with other surrounding themes, the digitally distributed news journalism that the young adults come across in their daily lives, often distributed as headlines published in social media, with its fact-based character, exemplifies themes with very narrow horizons. Schutz and Luckmann (1973) have theorised a distinction between the *inner horizon* of a theme, which only has room for the closest details about it, and the *outer horizon*, which establishes a relation between the theme and other relating themes. There is also the *total horizon* of a theme, which is practically unlimited and may lead to horizons far beyond the details that the theme provided in the first place (Schutz & Luckmann, 1973, pp. 193–195). 'The news', delivered as headlines in social media, stripped of meaning and context, can only be connected to the outer horizon by those who are already well equipped with knowledge about the event, and its social and cultural history and context. For others, with less education, life experiences or interest in world events, these short posts remain just information about, for example, a specific number of dead people, an attack that has struck somewhere or a strike in some remote place in the world. Similar ideas have been discussed by Regina Marchi (2012), who has argued that young audiences are sceptical about the concept of objectivity, and has pointed to "the need for news organizations to return to the original intention of the concept of journalistic objectivity, which was to disaffiliate news from public relations and propaganda, providing the public with information that would allow them to 'not only know but to understand'" (also Schudson, 2001, pp. 162–164)".

Searching for the outer horizon

It was already mentioned in Chapter 4 how our young participants often expressed a deep concern about the world and a strong and devoted interest in particularly one or a few 'my-topics' that they considered deeply urgent and existential, and as such significant for their identity and for them as human beings (for similar results, see also Clark & Marchi, 2017; Stald, 2023). To gain deeper knowledge about these – for the young people – existential topics, the young adults often turned to media formats beyond 'the news', such as podcasts, influencers and social media accounts of NGOs. Such broad information practices (see also Peters et al., 2022; Stald, 2023) indicate that youth today do not see news journalism as the most useful media format to establish links with the outer horizon of a certain theme, and that they find other kinds of mediated information more meaningful to take part of in their search for broad and deep knowledge about topics that they find interesting. Instead, their search for such knowledge take them to the mixed and multifaceted content in social media, podcasts, documentaries and other media formats. Daniel, the 26-year-old hairdresser that we have met before, for example, explained how he, after the killing of the African-American man George Floyd in May 2020, deeply felt he needed to understand more about the Black Lives Matter movement, after which he started to search for accounts on Instagram that "explained *in-depth* how darker people have been exposed, and what this is *actually* about", emphasising how social media added a cultural and historic contextualisation to how the event was described in 'the news'. A female Chemistry student, living in a wealthy suburb with her parents in a metropolitan area, in a group discussion proclaimed, unlike her friends in the focus group, that she did not have "one single important account, no politicians, no newspapers, no nothing" on Instagram, yet talked about how she sometimes clicked on links posted by influencers that she followed to get other people's opinions about various topics that she found interesting, and how she took part of others' discussions about news events, as a way of getting deeper information about the original event (Kajsa, university student, 21, metropolitan area). Watching documentaries on streaming services, listening to podcasts and following influencers were all put forward by the young adults as ways of deepening their understanding of certain topics and events that they had come across briefly in either news journalism or social media: their historical background, sometimes conflicting dimensions, and the broader themes surrounding them. A female university student in Political Science, for example, talked about how she had recently broadened her information repertoire for the explicit purpose of getting access to new, and "more *important*", information about societal issues that she did not get from 'the news'. This was exemplified by police brutality in the US, and the already mentioned BLM movement.

She described how she, as part of this attempt, had started to "update what I think is good information" and how she had added several new media formats to her media diet to get as broad and deep representations of these events as possible:

> I get a lot of information from Instagram, but I have also taken one step further and listened to documentaries that have been released. I may also have started to follow other kinds of accounts and other news media. But a lot of it is Instagram.
>
> (Hanna, university student, 22, university town)

'News' provided by social media was in this respect put forward as distinguished from 'the news' as it both broadened and deepened the information the young people received in 'the news' which could be used to get a deeper understanding of the world, also including a more personal, emotional, and human touch.

'News' on social media and the sharing of experience

We will now move on to discuss the third aspect of storytelling that Benjamin put forward, and that was also spontaneously brought up in the interviews by the young adults: its aspect of shared experience. Listening to a storyteller or even reading a story, Benjamin argued, is by nature *shared*, as "[a] man listening to a storyteller is in his company, even a man reading one, shares his companionship" (Benjamin, 1936/2006, p. 372). This feeling of not being alone, and the experience of sharing knowledge and information, was also spontaneously addressed in our interviews, for example by a young woman, studying to become a singer, who talked about how she got 'news' from varied feminist accounts in social media, particularly the 'search bubble' on Instagram, and how she got "*so* much information from Instagram, about the world, and my friends, and what is important *to other people*" (Jennifer, 23, student, metropolitan area). Sharing the experience of news could hence be linked to finding out how other people related to events that had happened. Another young woman stated that she had "a double approach to news, and the thing is that what I find interesting is to read discussions, and how ordinary people discuss" (Ylva, 20, care assistant, small community).

A gender-mixed group of 18-year-old gymnasium students in a low-wage suburb in a metropolitan area described that they considered Twitter to be "good because things are trending there that other people talk about". With the exception of a few, the young adults we talked to did not use social media to a large extent to express their own views publicly, but instead often followed discussions among others as an essential part of their own news practices. A male university student claimed he very seldom expressed his own opinions online, but said:

I often follow others who do it, on Instagram and so, who writes about their opinion. It's really exciting, I think. (...) Yesterday I read about [Swedish influencer] Margaux Dietz who has written a children's book about Africa with only white kids in it. I was very excited to hear people's opinions about that.

Interviewer: So, it's fun to take part of what other people share?

I find that really exciting, yes. I very seldom reply to it myself.

(Emil, 23, university student, university town)

Today, social media allow a plethora of voices to be heard, and the young adults often had an ambivalent approach to this. Few took an active part in open discussions online (although they sometimes discussed things that were important to them in closed groups or communities), as the price to do so was considered high. Ylva, the 20-year-old care assistant, preferred to follow the alternative internet forum *Flashback* to traditional news journalism as she found it more trustworthy due to the large variety of voices present there. She also underlined that she considered online discussions following from events publicised by 'the news' much more important to take part of than the information about the very event. She therefore often chose to check the online comments following a news event rather than information about the event itself, even though she sometimes considered it to be very emotionally demanding to do so (if the discussions were hateful and aggressive). When asked how she navigated her desire to know what other people were thinking about an event, in combination with her concern to not be emotionally hurt by the tone in some postings, she explained:

Sometimes on the news pages, there are these comments sections. Or ... if there's been a scandal involving a certain person, then it is like ... in social media you get really close to these people. Previously, you saw something on TV and then you did a lot of thinking, I mean, on your own, so to speak. But now you can actually go in and look at this person's Instagram. And get an immediate picture [of what has happened].

She continued to excitingly exemplify her reasoning with talking about a scandal that had recently occurred in 'the news', where a famous TV personality had been caught by the police when he paid a prostitute for sexual services (which is illegal in Sweden):

I just went directly to his Instagram. There I get his picture of what has happened ... and what everybody else is writing about it, and I kind of roll around in it all! It is as if 'the news' comes from TV, or from ... the authorities, and then everyone is gathering ... somewhere else and discuss it, *with* this person almost. It's such a ... weird thing [laughs] ... yea.

Interviewer: So that's kind of more interesting then, the discussion around it...?

> I think so, yes. Because the media ...or 'the news' gives you *one* picture ... and then there are lots of other pictures ... around it. They inform like this: "This has happened!" It's a bit like in school: "this has happened, now you discuss it in small groups". And then everybody runs to Instagram to discuss it [laughs]. ... Everyone is welcome!
>
> (Ylva, 20, care assistant, small community)

Hanna, the sociology student mentioned earlier, said that for her it was important to receive news from social media beside 'the news', as it both broadened and deepened her knowledge about things that had happened in the world, as well as sharing with her how other people related more personally to the events. Her regular information practices included a combination of 'the news' and 'news' she found online, as:

> Well, first to get broader information. And then, absolutely, it can be more personal, I mean, there is more of people's personal opinions in it, compared with ordinary news. News articles are a bit more professional, or how to put it. *Neater*, in a way. It can be that way on Instagram too, but often it is more personal, you can easily see their personal opinions.
>
> (Hanna, 22, university student, university town)

Daniel, the 26-year-old hairdresser, said he had a particular interest in conspiracy theories, and described how he tried to find information about such theories by googling or searching on varied online sites: particularly Instagram and the already mentioned alternative online discussion forum *Flashback*. Using the death of American businessman and suspected paedophile, Jeffrey Epstein as an example, he mentioned how he googled intensively and searched for hashtags related to Epstein to get more details about the case and what had been said about it. He made a clear distinction between *getting information* about what had happened, which he did not have any high hopes that he would get from these sources, and hearing people's *opinions* about it, and said:

> I wanted to learn more about it. Or 'learn' ... I don't know, but to hear some more stuff... *and see what other people think!* What if I'm not the only one who believes he was murdered in jail, by a lot of rich, political men, that he knew a lot of shit about? Or maybe he just committed suicide ...?
>
> (Daniel, 26, hairdresser, metropolitan area)

When discussing which sources he used most frequently to feed his interest in conspiracy theories, Daniel repeatedly came back to the role of the alternative site *Flashback*, that he saw as a prominent source of knowledge and a good way to learn more about "what others think, or believe, or so". He meant that *Flashback* provided him with the opinions of:

> Just ordinary people, like you and me, who sit down and write a lot of shit, really. But some-times it is fun to know if people think the same way as you do. When they try to explain something, even if we cannot know if that explanation is a hundred per cent true, that's up to you to check.
>
> (Daniel, 26, hairdresser, metropolitan area)

News journalism, as well as other sources of information hence filled distinctively different roles in the lives of the young – roles that they also articulated clearly. Ylva, the 20-year-old care assistant, repeatedly during the interview expressed pro-found scepticism of all kinds of news journalism, newspapers and journalists. When asked to reflect about, and develop, why she did not trust or relate to 'the news' she completely turned around and said:

> I do that *too*, of course. They have a lot of facts when they tell us about what has happened somewhere else. Of course! But it is as if, after I have seen something on TV or somewhere else, I just want to go [to social media] to see what other people *think* about it … or if people have a different idea about what has happened.
>
> (Ylva, 20, care assistant, small community)

The role of shareability in the meaning-making around 'the news' has been ad-dressed also by previous news research such as in Clark and Marchi's (2017) *Young People and the Future of News*, where they discuss the concept of 'connective journalism' as news in which young people may 'insert themselves into the story', and the audience is thus actively involved in the construction of the news event. Connective journalism explains how young people need to find a personal path into the news events and find it relatable enough to be shareable. Our young par-ticipants related to the shareability of news mostly as sharing both 'news' and 'the news' with smaller groups of selected individuals, as well as taking part when other people shared their opinions, yet this latter kind of shareability was often put forward as more interesting and worthwhile than engaging in the specific news event that started the discussion.

Conclusion

As we have concluded also in the previous chapters, many of our young partici-pants had a complex media diet that included a mixture of news journalism, social media, podcasts, documentaries and other kinds of content. A majority of them did not subscribe to a daily newspaper or watch the news on TV on a regular basis, but still came across 'the news' in social media or elsewhere. This means they often received 'the news' as short headlines and links that they had to click on to get the full news story, but which remained snippets as long as they did not do so.

The analysis of how the young adults discussed and related to 'the news' has particularly revolved around the futility and dreariness of news, as well as the disconnection of news journalism from the young people's own lives and the social contexts they inhabit and find meaningful. Both these dimensions can be understood by the relation between news as facts, events and storytelling, and the phenomenological horizon, meaning that which connects singular themes that we encounter with other themes and the broader historic and cultural context to which they relate. Tuchman (1976) early emphasised the dimension of storytelling in news journalism, and particularly how the journalistic transformation from events to stories made news meaningful to its audiences. Also today, storytelling, and particularly the lack of narrative dimensions of news, is sometimes put forward as one of the reasons why (young) audiences abandon news.

Following from the analysis presented here, we see that although Tuchman pointed to storytelling as an essential dimension of news journalism, a dimension which transforms news events from 'strips of reality' into something meaningful, the young adults we talked to, in opposition to this, mainly pointed to the straightforward, objective and factual dimension of 'the news' as its core element and raison d'être. Following from Benjamin's analysis of storytelling, we have learnt that what distinguishes stories from information is that stories are relatable, lasting and meaningful in relation to those who read them and their lives, while information (also including news journalism) hence is not meaningful in relation to people's lives in the same way. When the young adults articulated news as 'important and unimportant things', 'things that have happened somewhere else' or straightforward facts and information about past events, they also articulated that news journalism for them was often beyond what really concerned them. This, then, is an understanding of 'the news' which is quite different from the normative role of news as that which holds society together through a public connection.

One major transformation in the field of news journalism that has occurred since Tuchman formulated her thoughts about news as storytelling, and the role that journalists have in it, is the increasing automation and datafication of not only news production, but also of news distribution. Social media, as the main arena where young people today meet 'the news', have transformed the package of news from headlines followed by a story, to headlines alone, from meaningful content back to the 'strips of reality' that Tuchman (1976) meant was only the starting point for a good, and meaningful, news story.

As already mentioned in Chapter 4, such suggestions are supported by the study of young Danish news audiences, which points to the tech-driven and datafied distribution of news as one of the shaping factors behind young people's disinterest and, sometimes, disrespect for news (Stald, 2023; see also Aharoni et al., 2021). As our analysis has shown, news, when it is consumed mainly in social media, and curated based on datafied audience analyses, remains the strips of reality that according to Tuchman is only half of what news can and should be, to be meaningful. Such analysis also emphasises the role of craftmanship in storytelling, that Walter Benjamin emphasised, and that the digitised and datafied distribution of news today has seriously downplayed.

Chapter 7
Trust in news and information

While different forms of storytelling provided important resources to draw upon for the young adults, helping to make sense of the world and their position in it, their engagement with various media forms also foregrounds questions of trust, which will be the focus of this chapter. We have, so far in this book, discussed how a range of novel genres, often native to social media, were used as forms of hybrid news sources – and indeed as providers of meaningful stories – but the multitude of available media outlets, seen from another perspective, equally makes sound assessments of what is trustworthy more difficult. As noted in the introductory chapter, the spread of mis- and disinformation online has become a worldwide problem, affecting young as well as older media users, and further complicating discussions about trust in news and media in a multi-platform environment (Wagner & Boczkowski, 2019). Some scholars have, moreover, pointed to a perceived link between digitisation and blurring lines between 'expert' knowledge, shaped by professional and institutional actors, and more popular forms of knowledge, related to popular sensibilities potentially encouraged by alternative sources of news and information (Cmiel & Durham Peters, 2020).

In the chapter, we examine how young people talk about trust in relation to news and information that they encounter in their everyday lives, both concerning 'the news', as established news media, and 'news', conceptualised in broader ways. Rather than approaching trust as something fixed, or easily measurable, we focus on the way that they articulate and describe their experiences of trust (or distrust), examining what kinds of news and information the young adults say that they trust, and how they come to determine what to trust in their digitised everyday lives. We start by briefly overviewing theories and some current research on media trust, and then outline the young adults' own understandings of what sources of news and information they feel they can trust, and why. The second part of the analysis focuses on how they evaluate and compare different kinds of news and information, including that obtained on social media, while grappling with uncertainties and challenges when making decisions about where to place their trust. The last part of the analysis, finally, discusses how young audiences can meet these challenges partly by developing a range of micro-practices to evaluate different kinds of news and information, more based on personal experience and relationships. Overall, the chapter emphasises the intricacy of the subject; showing how young people may, on the one hand, have clear ideas about what types of news and information they should trust, but, on the other hand, may use a rather different set of evaluative practices when determining where to place their trust. Such tensions were also brought up in relation to established ideals about the value of being a certain kind of critical media user, which were often developed at school, and the difficulties of applying such ideals in practice.

Media trust and trust in news

The notion of trust is central to a great deal of scholarship on news and journalism. Social trust between people, as well as trust in institutions, can provide a ground for stability, democracy and cooperation, without which it would be difficult to build stable communities (Misztal, 1996). A certain degree of public trust, likewise, is normally thought of as key for the media to be able to function in their role as a 'fourth estate', keeping a check on those in power and providing information about important issues. Without a basic level of trust among citizens, getting such information across could potentially be made very difficult and from this perspective it is imperative for news audiences to hold a degree of trust, and to be able to do so on solid grounds. Yet, there is a great deal of concern about eroding trust in the news media, with a report from the Reuters Institute for Journalism, for example, starting from the idea of an erosion of this as a global challenge (Toff et al., 2020), which has also been related to a wider 'crisis of information' (Haider & Sundin, 2022), with information abundance and 'high choice' media environments creating new challenges for evaluating information. At the same time, trust in news media is contingent upon geo-political and cultural contexts, with somewhat opposing trends in different countries (Hanitzsch et al., 2018). It is also a complex subject to operationalise in research, partly as it has no agreed upon definitions.

Trust, overall, has been defined as an assumption about the future and as taking a risk without knowing the outcome (Luhmann, 2017), and, similarly, as "a bet about the future contingent actions of others" (Sztompka, 1999, p. 25), involving both beliefs, such as of reciprocity and benign conduct, and commitment through actions, such as making a choice based on those beliefs. Russell Hardin (2002) describes trust as "encapsulated interest": the expectation that the trusted party will have an interest in fulfilling the trust of the other. Discussing the subject from a sociological perspective, Piotr Sztompka, on the other hand, sees trust as a three-pronged category, involving a relational dimension, as a quality of a relationship; as well as a personality trait, a 'trusting impulse'; and finally a cultural dimension, meaning that the pre-existing cultural context has a bearing on decisions to trust or distrust (1999, pp. 60–68).

Public distrust in news media, as mentioned in the introduction, is often identified as a challenge for democracy, which is particularly prominent in some parts of the world, including in the US, where distrust in the news media has been related to factors such as polarised politics and a widespread belief that the news media have a political bias (e.g., Jones, 2004; Lee, 2010; Ognyanova, 2019). At the same time, 'blind' trust, accompanied by the inability to properly critique or understand the requirements of different news genres and formats, can be equally problematic (see Burroughs et al., 2009; Mihalidis, 2012). Distrust may also in some situations be a rational response, for example in authoritarian societies.[1] Some researchers, moreover, point to the difficulty in comparing studies of media trust, related to challenges in conceptually pin-pointing and operationalising the concept, as well as to the complexity of audience understandings, questioning its very usefulness in research (Fisher, 2016; Jakobsson & Stiernstedt, 2023).

As noted by Jesper Strömbäck et al. (2020, p. 140), 'media trust' and 'news media trust' are often used interchangeably. 'News media trust' may be a more precise term for examining audience approaches to news journalism specifically, usually referring to traditional news media such as newspapers, TV news and radio news – but this, too, carries a range of interpretations regarding both what is meant by trust and by news media. Providing a comprehensive review of literature on the subject, Strömbäck et al., however, find that much of this literature shares some basic assumptions:

> [A]t the broadest conceptual level, there is significant consensus that news media trust refers to the relationship between citizens (the trustors) and the news media (the trustees) where citizens, however tacit or habitual, in situations of uncertainty expect that interactions with the news media will lead to gains rather than losses.
>
> (Strömbäck et al., 2020, p. 141)

Starting from such an outlook, many recent studies about trust in news have examined trust in different forms of news journalism and news media (e.g., Kalogeropoulos et al., 2019; Strömbäck et al., 2020; Stubenvoll et al., 2021), looking at, for instance, levels of trust and distrust in digital news, as well as fake news detection in digital media (e.g., Blöbaum, 2016; Dabbous et al., 2021; Fletcher & Park, 2017; Livio & Cohen, 2018). Largely based on survey studies, certain overall findings appear to be corroborated across studies and countries, in that low levels of trust in public institutions and political systems seem to relate to low trust in the news

---

1 Sztompka provides an account of how democratic systems, by 'institutionalising distrust' in requiring justification of power through democratic checks and controls (such as periodical elections, divisions of power and open communication) paradoxically can produce spontaneous cultures of trust, whereas autocratic regimes institutionalise trust by formally demanding unconditional support for the rulers, with power based on arbitrary principle, and thereby producing a pervasive culture of distrust (1999, pp. 139–150).

media (Jones, 2004; Hanitzsch et al., 2018; Kiousis, 2001), whereas interpersonal trust as well as exposure to television news and newspapers positively correlate with media trust (Tsfati & Ariely, 2014), while the consumption of alternative news media can interlink with distrust in mainstream media (Jackob, 2010). However, as highlighted by Thomas Hanitzsch et al. (2018) in a comparative, longitudinal analysis of trust in the press in different countries, there appears to be little evidence of a unified worldwide trend towards a decline in public trust in news media.

A smaller number of recent studies have used qualitative methods to explore audience perspectives on trust in news and digital information more broadly and in relation to everyday practices and discourses. Erik Knudsen et al. (2021) investigate how the public describe news media trust in their own words, pointing, among other things, to the differences in worldviews and ideology among journalists and audience members, as well as underlining how a citizen perspective on news media trust is rarely explicated in existing research. Likewise, a multimethod study in Finland (Horowitz et al., 2021) stresses the notion of 'critical trust', meaning an awareness of the 'systemic' consequences of digitisation, especially the dangers of social media bubbles, disinformation and market-driven imperatives of journalism, as a prominent aspect of audience accounts, underlining a continual balancing between scepticism and trust in contemporary news consumption. Mapping such intricacies more specifically in relation to young people, Swart and Broersma (2022), based on a study of youth in the Netherlands, develop a taxonomy of young people's tactics when assessing the reliability of news (cf. Wagner & Boczkowski, 2019). The authors underline that young media users often employ pragmatic shortcuts to approximate the trustworthiness of news, including affective and intuitive tactics rooted in tacit knowledge.

Finally, Caroline Fisher (2016) makes an important point about how the long-held ideal of trust in news as a prerequisite for a well-functioning modern democracy has come to clash somewhat with the requirements of social media, while survey research from Norway (Enli & Rosenberg, 2018) has indicated that young people tend to trust political figures more when they appear on social media platforms than in traditional news media, also highlighting how trust in different media in this study related to the types of media that citizens were most used to, with younger people having higher levels of trust in content on social media compared with older generations. David Sterrett et al. (2019), furthermore, underline how opinions of news on social media are shaped not only by the content and credibility of the news but by the trustworthiness of the person who shares a story (cf. Ognyanova, 2019; Turcotte et al., 2015). Social media, then, seem to introduce new interpretive frames for determining whether or not to trust news and information, requiring extended critical capacities for doing so.

Views on trustworthy news

As we have discussed in previous chapters, the young people who participated in the study used a wide range of sources to obtain information about society, which often included some element of news journalism, although we have also seen how traditional news media were not necessarily central as providers of information about society and current events, as the young adults equally relied on influencers, video-logs on YouTube, content on Twitter/X, Instagram Stories, memes, podcasts, and postings of friends, family and others in their online networks, among many other sources. For some of the participants, social media, moreover, seemed to be crucial for finding out the goings-on in their near surroundings, as well as in the wider world. While the young adults were living in Sweden, their media habits, hence, in many ways reflected global trends in young people's news and media consumption (Newman et al., 2023, pp. 10–13).

When talking about what types of news and information they *trusted*, however, it was evident that there were certain sources the young adults generally considered especially trustworthy. In line with surveys and other research showing high levels of trust in public service media (radio, TV and websites) in Sweden (see Neuman, 2023; Stiernstedt, 2021), answers commonly highlighted public service media as particularly trustworthy and possible to turn to for reliable information about society or if something unexpected happened, with the public service television broadcaster, SVT, and Swedish Radio, SR, as well as SVT's news website, described as sources that most of the young people felt they could trust. "That's where you feel safe", as one 24-year-old media and journalism student living in a metropolitan area jokingly expressed it when talking about SVT and SR, whereas others described how they considered SVT especially trustworthy because of its perceived objectivity and balance, the journalists' integrity and for not advancing a particular political view. A group of male friends between 23 and 25, who lived in a university town in northern Sweden while studying music production and social science and working part-time in a shop and as a personal assistant, similarly described how they thought of "public service overall", including SVT and SR, as something that they trusted over other sources of news:

> Erik: I trust SVT a lot, if anything comes from them.
>
> Samuel: Swedish Radio.
>
> Erik: Yes, Swedish Radio. Well, public service overall.
>
> Alvar: I agree with you. I'm a bit more sceptical towards *Aftonbladet* and *Expressen* [tabloid newspapers] because I know several times when celebrities or, you know, half-known celebrities have spoken out about an article that was written and it wasn't true or it was written in

a way that was biased or distorted. Even if those newspapers are main papers and reliable for getting facts, in any case, I'm always a bit more alert there. But like you say, Patrik, I agree that *DN* [morning newspaper] and *SVT* ... those, I'm often less sceptical of, and normally I just simply trust what they say.

(Focus group, 23–25, university town)

As exemplified here, public service media were often compared to newspapers or to the TV channel TV4, which, alongside 'quality' newspapers such as *Dagens Nyheter* and *Svenska Dagbladet*, was also generally considered a trustworthy news source, whereas the tabloids *Aftonbladet* and *Expressen* were sometimes, as in this extract, discussed as more sensationalist and therefore less credible. However, as Alvar in this extract points out when saying that these newspapers are "main papers and reliable for getting facts", they could still, as established news brands, be trusted to turn to for fact-checking, or for reliable coverage of other areas, such as politics or world events. In some ways, then, it appeared that news media trust could relate to both the perceived integrity or intention of the source, as illustrated in views on public service, and to the established nature of the news media brand. Some of the participants likewise made a distinction between different journalistic genres and types of content when it came to what they trusted, with, for example, a Swedish online news site with a younger profile and a heavy proportion of celebrity news thought of as less trustworthy, with celebrity news an example of a genre which they generally would trust less. At the same time, certain less reliable sources or journalistic genres could be used for information that was interesting on an individual level but considered of less societal importance, and therefore enjoyed irrespective of its perceived truth-claim, as "it doesn't really *matter* if it's true or not", as Alicia, a 24-year-old previous business student living in a metropolitan area described it, referring to an example of a story about Beyoncés's engagement ring – illustrating how trust in news can be multifaceted and difficult to fully grasp in research.

Among the young adults that we talked to, there were also those who described themselves as having low trust in traditional news media. For example, one politically active 19-year-old, leaning towards right-wing politics, perceived Swedish news media overall as too "left-liberal" and generally not reflecting his viewpoints, whereas he felt that information found in social media, podcasts, international online media and Swedish right-wing alternative news sites offered him a broader perspective. The format itself did not matter in terms of trust, as it could be "an article, a video or a tweet", but such content outside of the mainstream media was considered "a complement" which he felt was otherwise missing. Another 18-year-old gymnasium student from a metropolitan area, who primarily used social media for news and information and said that he would "almost never" watch the news on TV, read a newspaper or go to a news site, expressed instead a general position of distrust regarding the news media as well as information found on social media, in stating that "you can't trust anything, really". He represented a sceptical stance that recurred in some of the interviews and focus groups and which, in relation to Sztompka's (1999, pp. 60–68) categorisation of the dimensions of trust, can be seen as relating both to 'a trusting impulse' as a personality trait and as involving social and cultural dimensions, where the social media context may be seen to potentially invite sceptical approaches. However, stances of general distrust or scepticism were also often nuanced within the discussions, as in this case when the same gymnasium student later reflected upon how he saw news journalism, after all, as "based on research" and therefore to some extent possible to trust, compared with information in social media, which he understood as more reliant on opinions and "feelings".

The young adults also referred to the integrity of the source when discussing the trustworthiness of other kinds of institutions and organisations, such as local and national government, ministries, tax authorities, state agencies and research institutions. Information provided directly by these organisations – such as health statistics during the pandemic – was often described as the most independent and trustworthy, and it could, in some cases, be regarded as a form of non-journalistic news. It also meant that some participants said that they at times preferred to sidestep news journalism and go directly to 'the sources' for information, as they trusted other information providers, for example NGOs or state organisations. As several of the interviews and focus groups were carried out during Covid-19, the website of the Swedish public health agency, Folkhälsomyndigheten, was repeatedly mentioned as a source that the young adults particularly trusted and would sometimes go to for updates on the pandemic. Yet, as illustrated by a group of friends aged 24–25 from a metropolitan area, of which one was a current university student and two had just finished their university studies in business and journalism, other government agencies, too, were highly trusted:

Interviewer: What do you trust the most?

Maja: The websites of government agencies. I mean, just Swedish government agencies, because I don't know about foreign government sites, if they're correct or not. But when it comes to this [Swedish government agencies], I feel that I can trust everything.

(...)

Elin: But, what I trust most is, of course ... the government agencies. Like, if I check the websites of [Swedish Tax Agency] or [Swedish Board for Student Finance]. Then I don't hesitate for a second [in believing them].

Later on in this discussion, Maja reflected further on how she felt that it was much more difficult to determine the trustworthiness of the websites of foreign government agencies, "to know whether it's correct or fake". Although some well-known international actors of a particular standing at the time of the interviews, including the World Health Organization, could be included in the non-journalistic institutions and organisations considered useful for 'news' updates and information, there was thus a distinction made between local and international sources of information in terms of trustworthiness. This was equally evident in other interviews and focus groups in relation to news media, where the young adults would often perceive Swedish news media as more trustworthy than international news sources that also appeared in their social media feeds.

While the discussions with the young adults made clear that there were some news sources that, by and large, were considered especially reliable and trustworthy, and that their perspectives in this way seemed to reflect their wider cultural context, it can be noted that these were not necessarily the news sources that they themselves used the most frequently, and sometimes not at all. For some, there thus appeared to be a certain discrepancy between *ideas* about what it was possible to trust and actual media practices; a dilemma that will be explored further in the next section.

"How do I know what to trust?" The challenge of evaluating sources

Even though some organisations and sources of news and information were viewed as more possible to trust than others, the participants equally explained how they, on an everyday basis, would often struggle with coming to terms with what was trustworthy among the flow of information that they would encounter. When using social media, they were not always aware of where different kinds of news and information would come from – as we have seen in Chapter 3 in relation to automation – or able to discern if a variety of user-generated content was credible or not. Many referred to the concept of 'source criticism' that almost all explained they had learnt at school, especially at gymnasium but also at university for those who were or had been students, as a valued tool to help them critically assess sources of information. "Since school, source criticism is part of my bone marrow", stressed 23-year-old Samuel from the group of friends in northern Sweden cited earlier, underlining how he felt it had become part of his identity as a media user and citizen, but also reflecting a national drive to incorporate media literacy in the national curriculum.[2] However, to apply this principle and critically evaluate sources could be challenging in practice:

> Interviewer: How do you determine what kind of sources are trustworthy and good sources of information, in your view?
>
> August: I think it depends on where the news comes from. If it's by a special person, a big celebrity, sort of, and that person posts it themselves, well then, you believe it. (…) But, then – I don't know if this is right – but the biggest news sites, like *DN*, that kind of thing, well I don't know about *Aftonbladet* but I guess I would trust it too. But if it's a site I've never seen before I really don't trust it. Then I google to see if someone else has written about it. Well, that's the kind of thing you really get to learn at school, this source evaluation, which comes up all the time.
>
> Lily: That's it, and when I went to university, we talked a lot about that, and it's not the easiest thing to do. But I guess the main thing is that, if you're not sure, to look at sources from a lot of different places and compare to see if they give a similar picture, to make sure that the news is true.
>
> Interviewer: OK …
>
> Lily: Well, it's …
>
> Interviewer: Perhaps difficult?
>
> Lily: Yes, it's time-consuming!
>
> (Focus group, 18–24, mid-size town)

As exemplified by this conversation from a focus group consisting of three siblings and the partner of one of them, living in a mid-size town in southern Sweden, academic knowledge about how to evaluate sources may not always be easily transferable to daily situations. However, these accounts interlink with the research of Wagner and Boczkowski (2019) and Swart and Broersma (2022) in underlining ongoing practices of 'trust-making' employed by young people in high-choice media environments, where, for our participants, media literacy skills learnt at school could be complemented with a range of other means of figuring out what to trust, and what not to trust.

Looking further into these instances of 'trust-making' in relation to the young adults' decisions on what to trust, it is important to point out, too, that there were discrepancies and inconsistencies in the material, where some participants used entirely opposing ideas and practices for coming to grips with what to trust from others. The following extract from a group of university students studying dif-

---

2 Jutta Haider and Olof Sundin (2022) provide an overview of how media and information literacy is incorporated in education in different countries, showing how the concept of 'source criticism' has an important role in Swedish schools.

ferent programmes in a metropolitan area, discussing how they feel about influencers and traditional news media from the perspective of trust, provides a pertinent illustration of the varied ways of thinking about trust:

Interviewer: What about the rest of you, do you feel like there are sources that you trust?

(...)

Erika: I feel like I need to read more articles to be able to answer that question. I read stuff with a bias from the right, as well as from the left ...

Interviewer: Could you exemplify what you read ...?

Erika: Well, it's *Dagens Nyheter* the most, and then *Aftonbladet*. Then I sometimes check *Nya Tider* [a right-wing, populist website]. (...) I actually think that everything is biased, and that there isn't anything that can be fully trusted. I mean, it's my opinion, and how I feel about what to trust. But if there's new stuff coming out I may read about it, and change my mind ...

Interviewer: (...) OK. Earlier we talked about influencers and people that you follow in your social media 'feeds'. Do you trust what you follow in social media?

Alina: Not at all.

(...)

Erika: No, but I mean ...Sometimes it feels like they're just over the top. And that can be good and bad. I do like it when influencers talk about, like, women's rights and things like that, I like that a lot, but then it can also become too much sometimes, I feel. (...)

Alina: Yes, and I feel like, with the internet, most people use their platform to be able to reach their followers with their views about things, their agenda, which is good. But some will do it just for the sake of marketing – they do get paid for this information, and irrespective of whether it's paid for or it's their own views, it's necessary to be critical and sceptical about what it is that they're saying. Because ... just because they have lots of followers and, like, do something that people look up to or are interested in doesn't mean that what they're saying are the facts and not worth checking. So, yes, I think that you should always be critical, to almost everything. Even if you know that the sources come from something credible and someone has a good intention with giving the information. ... So I think you should be critical to most things, actually.

Interviewer: But does that mean that you don't think there are sources that you feel like 'this source I always trust', or 'this is believable'?

Carl: I think, if I see the news, where they talk, what is it again – TV4? I think that I almost always trust them, or, actually, always. Because there's so much at stake when they're standing there, human to human, looking into the camera and telling their story. Then it's of course the case that there isn't a huge selection of news that they can have when they talk into the camera, which means that they really need to cover things that they know that 'this is correct'. I mean, articles that are published in, like, *Aftonbladet* or *DN* or *Expressen*, it can be thousands of articles, and there are some ... what are they called again, those people who write articles? That's right, there are some journalists who publish their articles there who may not have done all the research. And then there might be, I don't know if 'shit-posting' is the right term, but … erm … well, a lot that isn't true, according to me. But what is said in front of a camera, then there is a team who have come to an agreement that 'you can say this without being jumped on by people'. I feel that I have a lot more faith in that.

Interviewer: Is that because there is a bigger organisation behind …?

Carl: It's more that there is a lot to fit, sort of. An article, people can easily forget about it, but if someone sees the news [on TV] then they can trust it more because it's not as much 'shit-posting' on a newscast, as opposed to, what's it's called, *Aftonbladet*'s app, for example, (…)

Erika: Well, for me, just to add here … the thing is that, you know when it comes to influencers, I've felt that everything that's in front of the camera is just business, that's how I feel. And you can never know what's true or false, a lot of the stuff coming out has been false …

Interviewer: Are you now talking about influencers, or?

Erika: Exactly. (…) Well, I feel like they have to fake it, to get followers.

(Focus group, 20–23, metropolitan area)

In this extract, there is ongoing negotiation between different positions on what to trust and how to figure out what is trustworthy, ranging from the position that "there isn't anything that can be fully trusted" as "everything is biased", as held by Erika, to the understanding of news on TV4, a television channel, as reliable, while influencers are described as necessitating a critical approach due to their commercial nature. Carl's description of the way that he sees TV news as more trustworthy than printed news, moreover, is explained in relation to how a big TV production in front of the camera would be significantly more trustworthy than print journalism online, which, to him, appears more anonymous and more open to individual journalists to make mistakes. In this account, it also appears to be the visual aspect of the medium, a human "looking into the camera and telling their story", that contributes to the experience of credibility, aligning with a long history of film and photographic images as having a particular status as documentary evidence in Western history (see Cmiel & Durham Peters, 2020). By contrast, influencers' activities in front of the camera are, by Erika, felt to be "just business", designed solely to "get followers", illustrating, also, how the young adults often considered overtly commercial, sensationalist or attention-seeking media and content providers less trustworthy.

At the same time, commercial news media that were well established, such as *Aftonbladet*, the popular tabloid newspaper, could be perceived as somewhat trustworthy precisely because they were part of a big business, as the young adults, from this perspective, would see the commercial media system as a form of guarantee for a basic quality of journalism, as it would be in the organisations' interest to keep up a certain reputation and hold on to audiences. Here, the media system and the wider social context overall were seen to benefit good journalistic practices as "news journalists must do their job, otherwise no one will listen to them, and they will lose their position", as a 21-year-old care assistant living in a mid-size town expressed it. This did not mean they necessarily trusted journalists as a particularly skilled and truthful profession – although some did – but rather that they knew that journalists had to conform to certain ethics, or informal rules, which made them trustworthy. This journalistic ethos promised a certain independence among news journalists which made them reliable, according to the young adults in these discussions. Interestingly, they adopted a similar way of reasoning around their social media networks, where well-known influencers and other types of social media accounts with many followers were seen to have "too much to lose" to willingly provide false information, thereby being expected to provide correct information to their audiences.

A certain level of popularity could thus be viewed as strengthening the position of the source as trustworthy in the eyes of the young people, as companies, organisations and celebrities had to act and communicate responsibly and carefully in order to sustain the audience's attention and trust. Likewise, in line with how the person sharing a story on social media may impact on its perceived credibility (Sterrett et al., 2019), the *quantity* of people sharing the same type of information was also mentioned as an important measure in the evaluation of whether it could be trusted or not. For example, a group of 18-year-old gymnasium students in a less affluent suburb in a metropolitan area reasoned that if many people in one's network had shared something, some of these people must have checked the information, which could therefore be trusted. In part, these discussions therefore highlighted not only how more formal skills and overall understandings of news and information as part of wider media systems could be utilised as part of what we can think of as 'trust-making', but also how more tacit ideas of popularity and the role of friends and a wider network of contacts could come into play in these processes.

Seeking 'evidence' in experiences and relationships

Dealing with the challenge of knowing what to trust, then, could be handled in different ways, and evaluations could partly be based on the source's position in a macro-oriented media environment and the rules and mechanisms it was perceived to follow. Yet, as the discussions with the young adults progressed, more micro-oriented approaches became evident, related to seeking 'evidence' for trustworthiness in one's own experiences, relationships and feelings, or in the experiences of others. As noted, comparing sources could be one way of checking to see if something was a 'real' news story, but such 'fact-checking' could also relate to comparing facts in a combination of sources, of which some could be more personal – for example checking to see how a local news story had been covered in discussions on social media versus a news website – or relating the information they found to their own experiences, and basing their trust on their personal relationships with the people providing the information, be it people they knew and had met before, or 'unknown' journalists or influencers. These more micro-oriented approaches or practices, then, could be seen as fundamental to how the young adults handled the complexity of their media environment, and they are important to acknowledge for a fuller picture of how and why they trust certain sources.

In part, the discussions highlighted questions about the role that different kinds of social media may play for young people in their understanding of news and information, where previous research has underlined social media as a relational context for experiences of trust (Livio & Cohen, 2018). As noted, friends and contacts in one's networks could be important for the interpretation of certain news stories, but a range of other figures, that were looked up to or admired, also had a bearing on trust in certain news and information, including different kinds of celebrities and influencers. For example, one male participant explained how he liked to watch an American YouTuber for analysis of the situation around the pandemic, and that he found this character particularly trustworthy and knowledgeable on the subject, having followed the same person over a period of time. Building an ongoing relationship with an influencer or celebrity over an extended period, likewise, was described as creating a particular bond, which could strengthen the experiences of relating to a form of authority; someone especially trusted. However, there were also instances that illustrated how the relationship between influencer and follower can transform over time, alongside certain events or personal developments. This was exemplified by a 23-year-old female university student who was highly critical of certain influencers, due to earlier experiences of having trusted them on food advice that later appeared incorrect:

> When I was younger, I followed some influencers' idea of what veganism meant, which included never to cook with any food oil, as that was considered unhealthy. It became like a truth, they kept showing how to make daily meals without oil, and I did the same, for a long time. Two years ago, I started using oil in food again – and now I feel like a complete fool!
> (Jennifer, 23, university student, metropolitan area)

Perhaps as a result of the 'unbundling'–'rebundling' process of news in social media as discussed in previous chapters (Van Dijck et al., 2018, pp. 51–52), individual journalists, as also noted in the previous chapter, were rarely spontaneously mentioned, and many participants seemed to have relatively limited knowledge about journalism as a profession. The comment by Carl in the long extract intro-

duced earlier, about "those people who write articles" is a slightly extreme example but may yet illustrate a stance towards journalists as rather distant characters
in the young people's daily lives, as emphasised in the previous chapter. One exception to this was found in a statement by Yousef, a 22-year-old refugee mentioned in
the previous chapter, who had lived in Sweden for a few years and was studying
while being engaged in the local community, and who expressed admiration for
journalists and trust in their role as providers of knowledge and social service:

> I believe that those who work at *Aftonbladet*, the journalists who write, they have this knowl-
> edge. They have legitimation as journalists. And they've made a choice to go out in society and
> ... check what people believe, or what question is important in this society. They sit and write
> and publish in the newspaper because they want people to focus on what is currently hap-
> pening here.
>
> (Yousef, 22, gymnasium student, metropolitan area)

Although Yousef did not have personal experience of journalists, he showed a great
deal of appreciation for their work and role as providers of information and socially engaged professionals, with a potential link to the experiences of a refugee from
a context with restrictions on press freedom.

One vital dimension of finding 'evidence' for the evaluation of what to trust in
one's own experiences, relationships and feelings was otherwise measuring different kinds of content against one's own experiences, with participants referring to
their personal perceptions of a specific event when discussing if the media coverage of this was trustworthy or not. In the group of 18-year-old gymnasium students
mentioned earlier, the young adults talked about their understandings of there
being "huge differences when you compare the news to what is actually going
on in society", with one participant in this group explaining that "I live in the sub-
urbs, so I know the news media's reports are wrong". In a similar way, there was
an emphasis on the importance of having access to published links to original sources of information, to verify where the information was from. Even if few actually
said that they clicked on links to original sources, these were considered a sign of
trustworthiness that distinguished reliable information from less trustworthy
sources. Although most of the young adults seemed aware of the possibilities to
manipulate media content, visual media, photographs and videos were, nevertheless, recurringly emphasised as principally trustworthy, and were for example discussed in relation to events such as the Black Lives Matter movement. The imme-
diacy of social media production, felt not to leave much time to edit, interpret or
manipulate the content, could also serve as evidence of trustworthiness of social
media content, again underlining how social media constitute a specific framework for the interpretation of news and information in relation to trust (Sterrett
et al., 2019).

A related way of validating information concerned the personal experiences of others, judged both by the quantity of people sharing first-hand knowledge and the quality of the experiences these others claimed to have. One female participant, who talked about the Swedish alternative internet forum *Flashback* as a particularly trustworthy source, found the amount and variety of voices present there a clue to its trustworthiness. The experience of others was also discussed in relation to events that friends had experienced, and to unknown individuals and authorities, as discussed previously. Similarly, as we know from previous research, trust in news and information is also often referred to as 'a gut feeling' (Wagner & Boczkowski, 2019; Swart & Broersma, 2022) which was at times articulated by the participants here. A 24-year-old medical student reflecting on why she would trust certain sources, for instance, asked herself the basic question of "does it *feel* like they know what they're talking about?" Studying to become a doctor and consuming a lot of online content about physical training, she likewise said that she trusted influencers based on the way they moved, argued and referred to sources: "Some just do it better than others. They are just more reliable in the way they talk, and how they package their content" (Emelie, 24, student, metropolitan area).

Such quotes, then, illustrate the tension between rationality and intuition that can characterise the everyday struggles to establish what is trustworthy information in digital media, where style can be an intuitive dimension of the understanding of news and information in relation to experiences and relationships.

Conclusion

When talking about what they trusted as sources of news and information, and why, the participants in our study often gave nuanced accounts in response to such questions, and elaborated upon different ways in which they could be answered. It was clear that, for most, traditional news media, especially public service broadcasting but also more light-hearted television news on a commercial channel and the two well-established main morning newspapers, were considered to be trustworthy news sources, which the young adults generally felt that they could turn to if they needed reliable information. The two main tabloid newspapers were evaluated as somewhat more sensationalist and more eager to 'sell', but were overall also seen to be sites possible to turn to for getting 'the facts' in situations of crisis, which is in line with Strömbäck et al.'s (2020) definition of news trust cited previously. Interestingly, in these parts of the discussions, being able to get reliable 'facts' from 'the news', or knowing that it could be relied upon in times of need, could be seen as something that, in a similar way to how news media were often conceptually linked to ideas of a good society, was appreciated and valued. This somewhat complicates the picture painted in the previous chapter, and shows how complex the understandings of news and news journalism can be. Similarly, a common theme that was brought up spontaneously in the interviews and focus groups was the importance of being able to critically evaluate sources, which many said that they had learnt at school. These findings correlate with statistics about trust in different news brands, and could be seen as, at least partly, contextually bound, interlinked with the particular geo-cultural setting of Sweden and the national media available.

However, it was also apparent in the discussions about what to trust as part of their broader media use and day-to-day situations that making decisions around this could, on an everyday level, be highly complex. Many experienced it as challenging to know what to trust among the range of content available to them and especially in relation to social media, where the 'learnt' ways of assessing sources of information were not always applicable on a practical level. This was a dilemma in which it was possible to develop an overall scepticism, not really trusting anything, of which we saw some examples. But when evaluating different kinds of 'news' in social media, many had instead come to adopt other approaches for their 'trust-making', as an ongoing process, which relied on more intuitive, personal and experiential understandings and micro-practices, in line with previous research on practices for trust in information on social media. As part of these processes, the young adults searched for different forms of 'evidence' which made sense to them, to navigate and provide direction in a more uncertain environment, relying partly on personal experience, as articulated by themselves or by people they knew, or on personal relationships, which involved the coming to terms with what to trust in relation to known others, who could be friends or contacts in their networks, but also 'trust-making' as shaped in relation to an influencer or social media personality. These dimensions of trust in relation to news and information on social media, while only touched upon here, open up further questions about sense-making processes around trust in digital culture, underlining the complexity of the question of trust as seen from a young audience perspective.

Chapter 8
Navigating news in digital culture

This book has explored what news means to young adults today, how it is integrated in their everyday lives and how they use it to relate to the world around them. In the book, we have remained open to a broad understanding of news, including news journalism but also other forms of information and media formats that the young adults equally defined as news; looking at practices, interests, trust and varied kinds of sense-making processes. Based on this exploration, we may now conclude that although some aspects of news use in the lives of the young adults are new, others inform us about the many continuities in how news is experienced and integrated into daily habits, serving as a reminder of the importance of relating contemporary news use to that of previous times, not to rush to alarmist conclusions about the state of news, young people and the world. At the same time, a conceptual re-examining of news equally provides an opportunity to reflect on notable shifts in young people's ways of finding and getting access to information about the society in which they live, which partly seem to challenge the previous role of journalism in culture and society. In this chapter we will synthesise our analyses and discuss the broader implications and consequences of these findings in relation to our contemporary digital culture.

What is news?

Throughout the book we argue, in line with much contemporary research, that the concept of news is transforming, and that news, for young audiences today, encompasses more than just news journalism. In line with findings presented in Reuter's Institute for the Study of Journalism's 2022 report *The Kaleidoscope: Tracking Young People's Relationships with News* (Collao, 2022) we have argued for making a distinction between 'news', which comprises a broad range of information considered to be news by young audiences, and 'the news', which only includes news journalism. We hence support previous research that has pointed to a changed conception of news (Costera Meijer & Groot Kormelink, 2015; Swart & Broersma, 2023) and to young people's broadened 'information repertoires' (see Peters et al., 2022; Stald, 2023; Örnebring & Hellekant Rowe, 2022).

As our participants shared this idea of what news is, for them it encompassed a broad range of media formats and content. Information from influencers, friends, activists, or governmental authorities was often integrated as basic information in the daily media routines of the young adults, and these were hence considered to be just as meaningful, reliable, and relevant sources of information as news journalism, and often also talked about as news. 'The news', despite this, often held a special position in the *ideas* about information of (most of) the young adults, as it was generally considered trustworthy and safe, and as such a resource useful for brief updates on public issues, as well as an important source of information in times of crisis, when it was vital to get hold of correct and truthful information. News journalism, likewise, was often framed, in line with findings by other scholarly analyses, as a form of, albeit imperfect, public 'good', which citizens have a moral obligation to stay informed about (Hagen, 1992, 1994; Bengtsson 2007, 2012; Casero-Ripollés, 2012). This shows however, that for our young participants, news journalism was not necessarily *the* information provider, something which, as we noted in the introductory chapter, according to historical news research, if this were ever the case, it was during a short period in world history (Darnton, 2000; Pettegree, 2014; Hamilton & Tworek, 2017).

These changes in the perceptions of news also have implications for how the young adults related to, and engaged in, news. As shown in the previous chapters, the young Swedes did not look for relevant and meaningful information about the world only in news journalism, but in a wide variety of sources. In the 1970s, Tuchman wrote that news (journalism) is a "window on the world" (1978, p. 1) but the young adults we interviewed often preferred to use other kinds of information to explore and engage in their world. As their daily encounters with news and wider information about society take place in multifaceted media environments that can be characterised as 'hybrid' or 'ambient', in blurring the boundaries between information, news and entertainment, and providing a fleeting, 'always-on' experience involving diverse, individualised ways of communication and information-sharing (see Papacharissi, 2015, p. 29; Hermida, 2010), it becomes harder to specify where and how they access news, and where news comes from, with news use involving less discrete practices integrated into a totality of media use. Our analysis hence emphasises the value of approaching news use as part of this broader context, clarifying how news journalism can be an inherent, but not necessarily prioritised, aspect of an overall 'media day'.

One way that the young adults related to news was through what we have called 'my-topics' that have similarities with what Clark and Marchi (2017) have discussed as 'connective journalism'. My-topics is news issues that the young people were deeply engaged in, and hence eagerly searched for information about, and sometimes also shared information about on varied platforms, among friends, in groups, and in their social networks. News about such topics was interesting for them seemingly without spatial or temporal restrictions, which means it did not have to be geographically proximate, or even new to the world (only to the individual, or the people in his or her networks) to be interesting to engage in. Some of

the young adults' identities were heavily invested in these topics and our participants saw them as vital to who they were. 'My-topics' often related to structural
aspects of power in the world, including issues such as feminism, racism,
LGBTQ+ issues, and climate change, but could also involve less power-oriented issues such as the legalisation of cannabis. Although the interest in 'my-topics' does
not represent the only way of paying attention to and engaging in news among our
participants, the abundance of information from all over the world facilitated the
cultivation of their own personal news interests, allowing these interests to guide
their everyday news practices, including how they curated their own news feeds
across platforms. To make sure they stayed informed about their personal 'my-topics', the young people looked for information that was new to, and concerned,
them, which often included a deeper understanding of the topic, a historic contextualisation, structural explanations, and emotional connections.

The young adults' engagement in these existential and structurally urgent topics may also provide one key to a certain distancing from news journalism that
was often expressed in our interviews. These findings also resonate well with
Clark and Marchi's (2017) findings in *Young People and the Future of News.* Just
as the American teens that Clark and Marchi spoke to, our participants often considered conventional news to be a boring format, summarised as facts and decontextualised information about events in the near past (for similar findings see also
Hendrickx, 2024). Although, as already mentioned, news journalism in general was
seen as reliable and trustworthy – at least when it came to established Swedish
news outlets and public service media, but less so for some international news outlets – facts were considered uninteresting, available everywhere and as such not
"worth storing in your head" (Axel, 23, student, mid-sized town). Previous research
has suggested that the increasing amount of information in contemporary digital
culture leads to an information fatigue that keeps individuals from engaging in
'the news'. Experiences of information overload are notified in studies across
the world (Boczkowski, 2021; Schmitt et al., 2018), although we mainly found
such fatigue in relation to information that was considered less interesting, a category in which many of the young adults, although not all, included much of news
journalism. Clark and Marchi (2017) have pointed to the (lack of) narrative structure in news journalism as an explanation of why young people are downplaying it
to the benefit of other information formats, something which we to some extent
also saw among our participants. Especially when considering the specific 'my-topics', the restricted format of news journalism did not sufficiently meet, they
thought, their demands for depth, breadth, and emotional connection, even though
digitised news journalism holds the possibilities to link to older and more analytical articles in, for example, online newspapers.

In this book, however, we suggest a supplementary explanation of this (by some) downplaying of news, also relating to the digitisation of news journalism and the new ways of distributing and consuming news, particularly in social media. When sole facts are unbundled and presented as parts of headlines in short news posts in social media, without connection to the broader structures of the world – or, indeed, to the original context such as the full newspaper or the news programme – the young audience finds it less meaningful and hence also less relatable in relation to their own lives. After having heard of an interesting event in 'the news', the participants therefore often preferred to go to other media formats in search of a good story and a lasting value that they could make use of in relation to their own lives. This 'news', beyond news journalism, helped them to connect single news events to their own lives through its essential value and human touch, collectively constructed by a group of people, including a plethora of voices in longer and shorter posts, and as such also shared, and discussed, by people in their own personal networks that they trusted and felt connected to.

This way of seeing news as meaningful or not is often mistaken as individualised and centripetal, in the sense that news is only considered relevant if it is meaningful and relatable *from an individual point of view*, but the meaningfulness of news should, from our analysis of the young participants, rather be seen as relating to either themselves or to the people in their smaller or larger personal networks. This hence reveals that news is perceived as being relevant primarily from a relational perspective, revolving around the young people themselves, but equally around the people they cared about, and who were part of their networks. This conclusion is also based on some of the young audiences' intentions to curate their own news feeds in order to get information that they considered meaningful from their (and their networks') point of view, as they wanted news to concern their own, and the people in their networks', everyday situations, perspectives, needs and interests.

Although we have highlighted transforming ways of using news that, just as other recent research has shown, embrace a notion of change, it is also imperative not to overstate novelty. Ethnographic studies of news audiences, conducted in relation to television and print news, have for instance also found that audiences' definitions of news, also previously, differed from that of news producers (see Bird, 2010). Relating to this, we saw similarities between what kind of information the young people we talked to said they wanted to be updated about, and the kind of local news that young people found interesting in earlier media landscapes. The similarities in news interests between the young adults of today and young people in the 1970s, as discussed in Chapter 4, are noticeable and may in fact indicate that it may not be the news audiences that have transformed the most during the last decades, but rather the contexts in which news journalism are distributed and accessed. In relation to this it is here worth quoting Raymond Williams, who in the early 1960s claimed:

> We must of course not make the mistake of assuming that the only serious news is that classified as 'political, social and economic'; there are many other kinds of human facts which can be serious news. Yet The Press is so often discussed in terms of this one function, giving the facts necessary for political, social and economic judgement in a democracy, that it is worth noting not only the differences between papers, but the actual proportion in any and all.
>
> (Williams, 1962 pp. 42–43)

Williams's insights about the nature of newspapers in Britain in the 1960s invites us to consider that people go to other media formats today to find the kind of information that newspapers in previous media landscapes provided them with (such as sports, comics, local adds, etc.). Social media today often provides such content via a plethora of varied sources, in a breadth and richness that a single newspaper or news show on TV can never make room for.

News in time and space

The analyses of news practices and perceptions that we have put forward here both confirm and challenge what previous research has found. We have shown how the young adults' daily encounters with 'news' and 'the news' were often experienced as part of an automated flow, neither actively surveilled nor part of a conscious routine, which has led us to underline the notion of news as 'just appearing' as a notable facet of young people's news consumption; quite different from news or information 'repertoires' as at least partly more actively selected assemblages for gaining information, which have been emphasised in previous research on digital news consumption (e. g., Peters et al., 2022; Peters & Schrøder, 2018; Schrøder, 2015). This aspect of the young adults' encounters with various bits of news and information, relating to processes of automation, 'push notifications' and an algorithmic selection of content in search engines and on social media, highlight, we argue, a notable shift towards automation as fundamental to the overall spatio-temporal experiences of news in digital cultures. We also identified a discrepancy between the ideal of the informed citizen, based on the notion of an active orientation towards news journalism, and the practices the young adults adhered to, where social media played a critical role in their daily media routines, also contributing to frame practices around news and information.

When looking more closely at the digital news practices of our participants, we, again, see the same patterns as other contemporary researchers, particularly regarding the fragmented kind of news use that takes place in the 'interstices' of time (Dimmick et al., 2011), something we have identified as an *interval* news practice. Interval use of news is temporally and spatially scattered and takes place when an often short, empty time-slot appears during the day. Besides this, we however highlighted another contemporary news practice: *synchronal* uses of news. Synchronal news practices underline how news journalism and other kinds of 'news' are consumed synchronically, side by side with other tasks and media content, as they appear in the constant flow in social media. Datafied production and distribution of all kinds of information, including news journalism, allow people to encounter all kinds of news as small strips of content in their social media feeds, on Facebook, Instagram and TikTok, and to supplement and deepen their knowledge and understanding via YouTube, documentaries, podcasts, and so on, while doing something else. Synchronal news practices are hence a consequence of the possibilities to package and distribute, as well as to consume, news provided by digital, and datafied, technologies. Yet, we know from previous studies of media use in everyday life that people have always conducted parallel activities while reading a newspaper or watching the TV news (Bausinger, 1984; Morley, 1986; Bengtsson, 2007), and that the highly focused news consumer only accounted for a small part of the population in previous media landscapes, too.

A third kind of news practice that we have discussed is *ritual* uses of 'news'. This kind of news practice came up when we asked the young adults to describe, in detail, their media day, and their varied ways of navigating 'news' the way they did. Ritual uses of news, describing how the young adults, often in the morning, systematically went through their core selection of social, and other, media to be updated about what had happened while they were asleep, have significant similarities with how people have always used traditional newspapers, radio shows and TV news (Bausinger, 1984; Larsen, 2000) to get ready to meet a new day, and to move from the sheltered space of home to public space. Although the formats and platforms where news is distributed are different today, we can see that 'news' in a broad sense, often distributed in social media, takes on a similar role in the morning rituals of young people today, as news journalism did for people in previous media landscapes. Ritual uses of news, as articulated by the young adults, may seem to have similarities with what other scholars have identified as a routine practice of 'checking', or 'routine surveillance', in a multi-platform information environment (Antunovic et al., 2018), but we have here emphasised how the spatio-temporal conditions of such practices (such as being in bed, getting ready to move between different spaces) deepen its ritual meaning, beyond the pure scrolling or searching for information updates. One important difference between social media rituals and the news rituals in previous media landscapes is however that while the latter involved transformations from private to public space (Larsen, 2000), the social media rituals our participants took part in rather transformed them from unconnected individuals to relationally connected ones, enhanced by their media environments, accelerating connectivity (Van Dijck, 2013).

The young adults' broad ways of conceptualising news also transformed how they related to the temporalities of news as content, as particularly the newness in news was challenged. It was often not considered essential that news was new to the world, but rather to the individual person or his or her 'group', when navigating, taking part of, and sharing 'news'. Although some of the young adults emphasised the newness of 'news', as the young woman who claimed that "Kylie Jenner has a new lipstick, I didn't know that, that's news" (Kajsa, 21, university student, metropolitan area) 'news' did not have to be new to the world, as long as it was new to the individual. Instead, the temporalities of meaningful, or relevant, news could be both retrospective, introspective, and prospective.

We know from previous research that digital media have transformed how we relate to space. This is also true for news and its anchorage in physical geography. As discussed earlier, and in line with previous studies of news audiences (Dimmick et al., 2011; Peters, 2012; Van Damme et al., 2015), we have identified spatial practices of news that both confirm a more mobile and transitory spatiality, as news is practised 'on the go', as well as in the intervals between different tasks. Also, the geography of 'news' content, understood as the spatial anchorage inherent in news that the young people found meaningful to engage in, is structured differently compared with previous forms of news use. Traditionally, news relevance has been related to geographical and cultural proximity, between broader communities. Today, such proximity is more individualised and relates to the spatial experiences and connections of the individual news user, which makes it more dispersed and based on previous experiences and connections. Many of the young Swedes we talked to had travelled both within and outside of Europe and had their own individualised cosmopolitical approach to news (and the world), and some had also made friends through digital media across countries and continents. Some had parents who had immigrated to Sweden, or had moved there themselves, and had relatives and connections in other parts of the world. Many of them hence had their own relationship to remote places and the people inhabiting them, and looked for news and information relating to those places, letting their own experiences and connections frame how they related to both the geographical and cultural proximity of news.

News, world and life-world

The transformed ways news was spatio-temporally experienced, often connected to one's own position and relations in the world, indicates that the idea of *scale* is useful to bear in mind when thinking about why some news was considered relevant, and other news was not. Scale holds spatial dimensions, yet refers to a person's individual life-world, and what is phenomenologically included there. Berger and Luckmann (1966, p. 46) theorised this as the difference between consociates (those we meet face to face) and contemporaries (of whom we have only more or less detailed recollections, or know merely by hearsay), a difference described as a continuum of different degrees of anonymity (Berger & Luckmann, 1966, p. 47; see also Schutz, 1967). Barchas-Lichtenstein et al.'s (2021) linguistic analysis has shown that people's discursive constructions of news relevance relate to the scale of collectivities they subjectively belong to, something that our analysis also confirmed. This includes one's sense of belonging to a community, relating to previous experiences of places, connections to people inhabiting those places, and the consociates and contemporaries included in one's life-world. In practice, this means those who subjectively belong to larger-scale collectivities are more likely to find news relevant than those who feel included in smaller-scale collectivities (Barchas-Lichtenstein et al., 2021). This indicates a shift in how news is seen as relevant and meaningful, from relevance constructed in relation to a public sphere of unknown contemporaries, to a relational relevance, relating to the individual and his or her consociates.

Another way our participants considered news relevant was interest-oriented, which means they paid attention to news if it related to their own personal interests (regardless of its general newness or spatial proximity). Such findings also correlate with Clark and Marchi's (2017) findings, that young people want to insert themselves into the news story. In the book, we discuss these issues as 'my-topics', relating to structural aspects of contemporary power dimensions, such as climate change, racism, feminism, LGBTQ+ issues, and so on. 'My-topics' were seldom of immediate, but more structural, urgency but worked as a continuing framework when navigating 'news', above the humdrum of current events. Our participants looked for information about these topics across both traditional news media and varied social media platforms, as they often considered the information they found about these topics beyond 'the news' to be richer, deeper, more interesting and emotionally engaging.

Previous research has pointed both to the abundance of information and the depressing character of news as possible explanations of why news audiences may turn away from 'the news'. We see similar tendencies, as several of our interviewees also referred to the negative character when explaining their disinterest in news journalism. An even more salient discourse about news that emerged, however, was that it was perceived as boring (c.f. Hendrickx, 2024). News journalism was often described simply as information about facts and events provided in a stream of data which may be meaningful in particular situations, especially in crises or other unexpected societal situations when certain and immediate information is needed. When they needed such information, the participants knew where to find it, and they appreciated its societal significance, but it did not necessarily play a pertinent role in their day-to-day lives.

Our participants also expressed how they missed a human voice, as well as a *variety* of voices, in digitally distributed news journalism, something they instead looked for in social, and alternative, media such as varied discussion forums. When explaining in their own words why they found 'news' in social media more engaging than 'the news', they also underlined their personal relationships with influencers and other individuals who shared their opinions and emotions online, compared with the more professional ("neater" as Hanna, 23, a university student in a university town, put it), but also less personal, news journalism. This, then, indicates that the weakened role of journalists in the production of information, in the wake of new technologies and technological professions (Westlund & Lewis, 2014; Vulpius, 2023; Zelizer et al., 2022), has contributed to eroding the relationships between news journalism and its audiences. As new professionals have entered news production and have taken more prominent roles in the analysis of audiences and the production and distribution of news, the human relationship connecting journalists to their audiences seems to have been undermined. This allows audiences to rather look for information from people they can connect to, such as influencers, activists, and celebrities, seemingly blurring the lines between 'expert knowledge' and popular forms of knowledge (Cmiel & Durham Peters, 2020), as considered in Chapter 7.

In relation to this we have also looked at the perception of news as events and stories, where stories were approached as something wider (and deeper) than their narrative structure. Stories, and storytelling, we argue, following Walter Benjamin (1936/2006), are about meaning, usefulness and a lasting value, something the young adults did not particularly associate with 'the news'. We related these discourses about news journalism to the digital distribution of news, as most young people today meet 'the news' in social media, which means they receive it as small fragments of stories, told by an anonymous voice, and without the 'outer structure' that connects single facts to the broader structures of the world, obviously of interest for many of the young. Algorithmic distribution of news is said to personalise it, yet our young participants mainly related to news flashes in social media as fragments of information, that few felt concerned them, and hence engaged in enough to get the full picture of the story. Elizabeth

Bird (1992; c.f. Johansson, 2008) early showed how news media in previous media landscapes used to provide people with stories they needed to navigate the moral, cultural, and social dimensions of life, and to situate themselves in society, something our participants often turned to other media formats to do. This may thus support Walter Benjamin's suggestion that information society, particularly the aggressive digitisation and datafication of contemporary news journalism, has destroyed (news as) storytelling, as his early doomsday prophecy suggested. This means that the tech-dependent and datafied production, distribution, and use of 'the news' strips it of meaning, or reshapes it from stories to events, to use Tuchman's (1976) terminology. Such interpretation may also propose that news journalism's role in maintaining people's public connection is declining, as, among the young people we talked to, social (and other) media held a more prominent position in keeping them connected to their own personalised networks and the matters of relevance there.

As we discussed in the introduction to this book, contemporary discussions about the public sphere often discuss its transformations in horizontal terms (as fragmented, by filter bubbles, etc.), suggesting that people gather in parallel formations of smaller publics, built around their personal interests. We see this in our material too, as our analysis shows how people share news in micro-communities, rather than in public space. As we have developed in relation to the sharing of memes in Chapter 3, such communities may sometimes be regarded as a form of 'micro-publics', which in some instances function to orient people towards public life (c.f. Clark & Marchi, 2017, p. 116; Swart et al., 2018).

Linked to this is however also the way our participants conceptualised the information they came across as 'small news', 'big news', 'my news' and 'news of the world'. Big/world news was discussed as events that are always, but not only, covered by news journalism, while my/small news as issues sometimes covered by news journalism, but most often not. This distinction seems similar to the distinction between local, domestic or international news, but the phenomenological distinction between 'world' and 'my' news is significant from a life-world, rather than a geographical, or cultural, perspective. 'My' news was seen as meaningful from either an individual perspective, or from the perspectives of the people in one's networks, ranging from very practical everyday life tasks, such as bringing an umbrella or not when leaving home in the morning, to negotiating moral dilemmas, as well as one's (or one's consociates') relation to broader power structures and global challenges. Worth noting is that 'world news', or news journalism, was in these discussions talked about as something separate from 'my world' and was, due to this, often seen as less meaningful, and useful, information. The distinction between world news and my news, big news and small news, is worth taking a closer look at. When conducting the very first interview of our project, involving four young people studying at different programmes at the university, we did not know how many times we would come across similar ways of talking about 'the news' that Carl (21), a student at a game design programme, frankly shared with us:

> Interviewer: How often do you for example read, or take part in, that kind of traditional news sources?
>
> F: Very seldom.
>
> Interviewer: Okay and what does that mean?
>
> F: I'm simply just tired of it. I used to be very active, or 'very active' [shows quotation marks with his hands], but I actively followed three different news sources just to, you know, update my flow. Then I was just sick and tired of it, after I finished high school, and I thought, "if I read, or if I don't read, it will not make any difference to the world". So, I just stopped, and I follow stuff that makes me happy instead. And that is watching people who motivate others, in physical exercise or design, or things that will affect my work life in the future.
>
> (Carl, 21, university student, metropolitan area)

The idea that Carl put forward, about 'the world' as something disconnected from 'his world', is a discourse that came up in varied ways, but repeatedly, during our fieldwork. World, or big, news, meaning news journalism, was in these discourses expressed as important for 'the world', being "about important and unimportant things" or "about somewhere else", and yet also seen as less meaningful news from the individual's own point of view. Such discourses may indicate a widening gap between what young people perceive as their world, and the world of 'the news', although there were obviously differences between individuals. Some felt they belonged to 'the world' of 'the news' and wanted to know about, and understand it, while others considered both 'news' and 'the news' worthwhile paying attention to only if it concerned them and the everyday world they perceived as theirs.

Taken together, this indicates that as (young) people in their everyday lives are flooded with decontextualised data, they restrict their use of information to those areas that engage them and the people in their networks, and that they find *useful* for navigating 'their world', in areas where this is possible. Many of our participants seemed to consider 'their world' equal to their own everyday lives, and the lives of the people they were connected with, yet also including structural dimensions of power that impacts directly on this (such as feminism, racism, LGBTQ+, etc.). In that sense, the way they pay attention to information has more in common with a Dewean (1916/1923) conception of a public, seen as consisting of a group of people "who regard themselves as likely to become involved in the consequences of an event, and are sufficiently concerned to interest themselves in the possibility of control" (Shibutani, 1966, p. 38), than the idea of a universal Habermasian public sphere and linked discussions of public connection (Couldry et al., 2007b; Hovden & Moe, 2017; Kaun, 2012). A public in the Dewean sense is hence identified in terms of its common focus of attention and concern, where news is not simply information packaged in a certain format, but information *that is important to someone* (Shibutani, 1966, pp. 38–40). According to such approach to the public, it is characterised by a conversation around a certain issue or problem that requires a collective response, and is in this sense more unformal, ephemeral, and less organised than the Habermasian notion of a public sphere. This way of understanding the public also sees it as a collective behaviour that is neither centrally organised nor directed by a shared objective, or formal rules (Dolata & Schrape, 2016). A Dewean public is rather formed and acted out by way of the relations between its participants, building primarily on a joint relationship to, and interest in, an event or a societal question of urgency. 'My news' and 'my-topics', as ways of forming publics in this other way, are in this sense distinguished from 'the news of the world', which our participants often articulated as something that did not concern them, something which suggests that a broader conceptualisation of 'news', beyond news journalism, does not does not necessarily enhance a public connection, but one that can primarily be relational.

In the introduction to this book, we introduced news as something traditionally seen as a commodity produced and packaged within organised journalistic institutions, involving, among other things, an emphasis on newness, a truth-claim, a specific tone and a set of particular values and actors determining what is newsworthy to an audience (e. g., Galtung & Ruge, 1965; Gans, 1979; Tuchman, 1978). Synthesising what we have discussed in this book – concluding that young audiences' perceptions of 'news' differ both from that of news journalists, but perhaps also from how audiences conceptualised news in previous media landscapes – our analyses point to the need for an audience-centred definition of news, as 'news' from the young adults' perspective both relates to other spatio-temporalities than 'the news', and revolves around other kinds of information: information that audiences see as essential when navigating *their* life, and that has an impact on *their* world, and is as such *meaningful* for either them or the people in their networks. Based on this, we here make an attempt to formulate an audience-centred definition of 'news', for news in digital culture:

> News, from an audience perspective, is media content that people find vital to understand and manage their lives, to keep connected to, and stay updated about, aspects of relevance to their life-world and those inhabiting it, and for making an impact on matters of perceived agency. News is provided by a plethora of sources, in varied media formats, and offers a combination of useful information, emotions, understandings of, and connections to, the their world.

As expressed in this study of young audiences in a particular geo-cultural context, 'news' is hence rather seen as a window to *one's own world*, defined by one's own life-world (including those who inhabit it), constructed at the backdrop of the scale of collectivities one feels a belonging to, and in which one perceives one has agency, rather than to 'the world' as suggested by Tuchman (1978). Some of the young people we talked to felt they belonged to the public world of 'the news' and hence engaged in news journalism, while others, as Carl quoted above, just wanted the kind of relatable daily 'news' they felt concerned them.

News in digital culture

Although we, in this book, have underlined findings that tell us not to jump to alarmist conclusions about transitioning news interests and use, we have also pointed to some novel aspects of news in contemporary digital culture that are worth exploring a little more in depth. The first aspect regards the idea about society as 'layered', consisting of a 'big world' and a 'small world'. In our digital media culture, both 'news' and 'the news' are flooding (young) people's everyday lives in mainly, but not only, social media. Some of our young participants used, often social, media to broaden and deepen their knowledge about public issues in the world as a complement to news journalism, while others preferred to stay updated only about 'news', as a broad genre, that they considered relevant in 'their world', as it was considered meaningful for, and impacting directly on, them, or the people in their digital and analogue networks. This confirms that despite the accessibility of information today, people perceive differently how news and information are actually for, and about, them, depending on what they consider to be the boundaries of 'their world'. This also underscores that news and information, according to the young adults, ought be *relatable for them, in one way or another*, to be meaningful.

The second aspect regards the role of news and information as something which connects an individual not necessarily to the public sphere, but to their own personal networks. Such networks, as mentioned, are constituted by people one has a close relationship with and meet and speak to often, as well as for example influencers and celebrities that one has established a relationship with, but that one may have never met. Such possible shifts in the role of news are visible for example in ritual 'news' practices, where news research in pre-digital media times showed how people used the morning news to ritually transform from private to public space, whereas our participants engaged in their 'news' rituals to transform from the position of a single individual to a *relational* human being, updated and connected to the network's current status. We also see this tendency in how our participants constructed news relevance, stating that news was mainly relevant if it was meaningful in relation to everyday matters that concerned them or the people they cared about as well as to broader structural aspects of society which also profoundly affected their daily lives (such as feminism, climate change, LGBTQ+-issues etc.). When broadening the concept of news the way our participants do, 'news' is hence meaningful mainly from the perspective of a relational connection, rather than the public connection that news journalism is considered to provide.

The third aspect regards the temporality, and *newness*, of news. Although the newness of news often came up in discussions with our participants about what news is, this newness was individually constructed, rather than related to when the piece of news was published, when it was new to the world. News was also prescribed a kind of newness if it was possibly new and interesting to individuals or groups in one's personal network, and hence worth sharing with that individual or (selected) group. This also points to the newness of news as a relational aspect, rather than relating news and the news user to a public discussion, also considering the many different temporalities inherent in the relevance of news. Based on such conclusions it is possible to point to how the digitisation and datafication of news have profoundly changed the temporalities of news and information, from an emphasis on futurity (and collective newness), along with what Taina Bucher (2020) has identified as the *kairos* of digital media temporality, emphasising the *appropriate time*, characterising algorithmically governed digital media. This temporal 'appropriateness' is characterised by crucial moments, rather than a linear development of time, and implies, Bucher means, a more personal notion of time (2020, pp. 1701, 1707). When it comes to digital news, then, this 'kairologic' includes both how varied news providers use algorithms to deliver content that is supposed to feel right and timely according to what goes on in a person's digital networks, but also how individuals navigate what content they will pay attention to, based on what feels right *in that moment*, as algorithmic right-time is both "variable and context-dependent" (Bucher, 2020, p. 1709). Ideas about 'news-finds-me' perceptions (De Zúñiga et al., 2017; De Zúñiga et al., 2020) may hence be understood in the context of an 'algorithmic right-time', where media users are assured that they need not be updated about the latest news when it is new to the world, as they can rely on digital media to deliver the most relevant updates, when the time is right for them. This, it has hence been argued, also underscores the *kairos* of digital media as a personalised time regime, rather than a common public time (Bucher, 2020, pp. 1709–1711; see also Kaun & Stiernstedt, 2014). Based on our discussion here, we would however argue that the *kairos* of digital 'news' is more *relational* than personal, as the temporality of news in digital culture is constructed by what is going on, and is shared and discussed, in one's social networks, as when choosing what news to pay attention to, or share with others, people navigate whether specific 'news' is relevant to engage in or not according to the way it may be new, and meaningful, for either themselves or for the people in their networks. Such novel, and relational, temporalities hence deeply challenge the traditional notion of news as something which is common, new to the world, and future-oriented, and contributing to discussions in the public sphere. News, as it is constructed by the young adults here, delivered as a flow of information and adjusted to a relationally organised algorithmic right-time, may again underscore Shibutani's suggestion that news is not mere information, but information that is important to someone (Shibutani, 1966, p. 41), *right here, right now.* Another temporal dimension of the distribution of 'news' in social media, following the logics of an 'algorithmic right time', is that its synchronising dimensions have been deeply transformed. Benedict Anderson put forward synchronisation as one of the features of news that helped create nation states as imagined communities (1983/1991), and hence also as spheres for public discussions. As has been pointed out by Jordheim and Ytreberg (2021), social media do not synchronise nations, but *networks* of people, which means that as both 'news' and 'the news', particularly for young people, are mainly distributed and consumed in social media, and as people engage in news when it suits their interstices in everyday life, synchronally with other media content, and framed by the interests, practices of sharing, and discussions in their own personal networks and news feeds, both 'news' and 'the news', in a social media context, synchronise people's *networks* and not entire nations or public spheres.

These three aspects, the *temporal, relational* and *layered* dimensions of news in digital culture, imply that the profound digitisation of society and culture may have taken us towards a new information regime, recalling a pre-modern structure of distribution and use of mediated information, at hand before the printed word dominated societal communication, and hence also society (c.f. Dewey 1926/1923). In his ground-breaking work *The Invention of News: How the World Came to Know about Itself*, Andrew Pettegree (2014) paints a picture of the information culture in medieval Europe, before the emergence of common print culture and a professional news market, that in many ways resembles the 'news' culture that we have discussed in this book. News and information then, were also highly relational. Those who wanted access to safe, reliable, and predictable information either had to pay large sums to build up a personal information network of their own, something which only people of utmost wealth could afford, or they had to rely on those who under a social obligation provided news for free. Professional news was mainly about events of importance for Europe's rulers, while most of the people relied on news they could get hold of for free, in the tavern or marketplace, or in official announcements proclaimed on the town hall steps (Pettegree,

2014, Chapter 1; see also Darnton, 2000). Side by side with the emerging news market, an abundance of rumours about a variety of topics emerged around everyday matters of smaller or larger scales: "who was to marry whom, which merchants and tradesmen faced ruin, whose reputation had been compromised by a liaison with a servant or apprentice" (Pettegree, 2014, p. 4). Even after the emergence of the news market, most people continued to receive much of their news by word of mouth. Pettegree states:

> [O]ur medieval ancestors had a profound suspicion of information that came to them in written form. They were by no means certain that something written was more trustworthy than the spoken word. Rather the contrary: a news report gained credibility from the reputation of the person who delivered it. So a news report delivered verbally by a trusted friend or messenger was far more likely to be believed than an anonymous written report. This old tradition, where the trust given to a report depended on the credit of the teller, had an enduring influence over attitudes to news reporting.
>
> (Pettegree, 2014, p. 4)

We do not see the same kind of outspoken suspicion towards written information as expressed by the people in the Middle Ages, although, as discussed in Chapter 7, our participants did put forward visual media as particularly trustworthy and reliable, and many grappled with everyday decisions about what kind of information to trust in social media. Instead, our participants mixed written, oral, and visual formats in their news practices, but regardless of communication form, they underlined the importance of a connection with the person providing the information, such as an influencer, friend or acquaintance who they often preferred to the distant, 'neat' and 'professional' voice of news journalism. This underscores the connections between the way our participants related to 'news', emphasising its relevance for the people in their networks, and their own personal connection to the person that provides them with it. Just as today, 'news', in the Middle Ages, included a plethora of voices delivered as, for example, pamphlets, newsletters, ballads and rumours, a diverse mixture of information that was available to anyone, compared with 'professional news' that was only for an exclusive elite (see also Conboy, 2002).

Historian Peter Burke has conceptualised this way of structuring culture in medieval times in *layers* as 'the great' and 'the little' tradition (Burke, 1978/2017). Although there was an exchange between 'the little' and 'the great' tradition, Burke says, the 'great tradition' was exclusive to the societal elite, while the 'little tradition' was accessible to anyone. These two cultural layers coexisted harmoniously in society, while also creating sharp lines between the people who had access to both traditions, and those who had access to only one of them. The way some of our participants relate to news and information, in a world of information abundance where everything is available to anyone at any time, but where many of our participants did not consider news journalism to be about and for them, also constructs the world as layered, where 'big news' was considered relevant to the world, and 'small news' relevant to them. The differences between the young adults in this respect, where some felt truly integrated in 'the world of the news' while others did not, supports Barchas-Lichtenstein et al.'s (2021) suggestion that people's engagement in 'the news' (and in 'news') relates to the scale of collectivities to which they subjectively belong.

There are of course huge differences between the medieval information landscape and that of contemporary Sweden, as Sweden is a highly digitised, well-functioning and wealthy democracy, where every citizen has access to, and often also trusts, public service media, and other news media. Nonetheless, few of our participants considered it essential to, in their 'media day', take part of professionally produced news outlets to navigate and manage their world, and instead valued informative media content (sometimes including news journalism) that was posted and shared by ordinary people, and they also preferred to share their own personal experiences and opinions in their own smaller networks, rather than in open forums. Another key dimension, hence, relating to the construction of relevant news, is *trust*, where our participants, while placing a relatively high degree of trust in traditional news media overall, viewing it, for example, as something reliable to turn to in a situation of crisis, often in their mundane social media use trusted information either based on their own experiences, or the experiences of people they knew personally, or with whom they had a personal relationship. This also recalls of the distribution of news in the pre-modern era, as then, Pettegree reminds us, news was mainly "a private and intimate transaction, exchanged between trusted individuals" (2014, pp. 96) and trust was hence built on the individual relationship between the person delivering a piece of news and the one receiving it. With the professionalisation of news and newspapers, such ways of trusting were later transformed into the more abstract trust of modern society, where people learnt to trust not individual journalists, but the journalistic system as such. Taken together, these dimensions: the layered worldview, the relational construction of one's life-world and interests, and of constructing trust – and what is hence seen as relevant and meaningful 'news' – also in many ways correspond with the ways that information was provided, used, and made sense of in pre-modern society. The correspondences between contemporary digital culture and pre-modern news culture underline what internet historians have called the 'restoration topos', taking a medium theory approach (McLuhan, 1964/1994; Ong, 1982/2002) particularly building on the idea of a primary and secondary orality (Ong, 1982/2002, pp. 136–138). The 'restoration topos' suggests that we "are in the process of closing a 'Gutenberg Parenthesis' in the history of media technology:

a period of four to five centuries in which the mediation of verbal culture has been dominated by print technology in general and the printed book in particular" (Pettitt, 2013, p. 55).

The 'restoration topos' means today's techno-cultural condition has more in common with cultural production and consumption of the pre-print era than with the age of print (and printed newspapers). Such argument suggests that the rational autonomous selves emerged in conjunction with literacy-print while "the rise of electric media – beginning with the telegraph, radio, and then movies and TV – correlates with an apparent shift towards more strongly *relational* – and almost certainly more *emotive* – senses of selfhood" (Ess, 2014, p. 626). Our analysis of the young adults' news practices and perceptions, what they consider relevant and decide to trust, may not entirely support the idea of a restoration topos, but shows that the logics of print culture today seem to reside side by side with the features of oral culture, and not only an orally, but also a visually dominated digital culture (see also Pettegree 2014, pp. 371–372).

Navigating the future

When Julia, whom we introduced in the first chapter of this book, has finished her morning ritual, she has got a grip on what the people in her social networks are up to, what they have been doing during the night and morning, what they engage in and discuss, and whether there is new information regarding areas that she is interested in, that she should get updated on. On an ordinary morning, she does not really know what is discussed in the newspapers, but if there has been a major news event, it is likely to have been shared by someone in her networks, and it would hence have come to her attention. She is ready to meet a new day, during which she will be accompanied by her mobile phone most of the day, and stay updated with what her apps and networks in social media provide her with. In this sense, her social media networks define much of what she knows, and synchronises the information she is provided with, with that of the others in her networks, which may be individuals, but also media houses, organisations, activist groups, organised by an algorithmic *right time.* Social media in this sense keep her connected to what is going on, what is considered important, what is discussed and debated in these networks, rather than in the public sphere. The news practices of young adults that we have discussed in this book do include dimensions of public connection, but those of our participants who mainly engaged in news and information via social media, were rather connected to their digital networks, as these media synchronised their world according to the network, and those included there.

We do not know what will happen when Julia grows older, when she may move on to university, get a stable occupation, perhaps have children and raise a family. It is likely that she will change how she relates to the world, what she considers important in it, what she wants to contribute to, and what means she feels she can use to engage in such contributions. Maturing is a process when most people take responsibility for more than just themselves, and it is therefore likely that the interests and practices of Julia, as well as of many of the real young people who generously shared their ideas and thoughts with us during our field-work for this book, will change as they grow older. Yet, we know that media practices established during the formative years are likely to settle as people grow older. It is therefore urgent we further explore what the synchronisation of news, in digital culture, means for people's connections to the world.

References

Aalberg, T., Blekesaune, A., & Elvestad, E. (2013). Media choice and informed democracy: Toward increasing news consumption gaps in Europe? *International Journal of Press/Politics, 18*(3), 281–303. https://doi.org/10.1177/194016121348599

Aharoni, T., Kligler-Vilenchik, N., & Tenenboim-Weinblatt, K. (2021). "Be less of a slave to the news": A texto-material perspective on news avoidance among young adults. *Journalism Studies, 22*(1), 42–59. https://doi.org/10.1080/1461670X.2020.1852885

Alasuutari, P. (1999). Introduction: Three phases of reception studies. In P. Alasuutari (Ed.), *Rethinking the media audience* (pp. 1–21). London: Sage.

Almgren, S. M., & Olsson, T. (2015). "Let's get them involved"... to some extent: Analyzing online news participation. *Social Media + Society, 1*(2), 1–11. https://doi.org/10.1177/2056305115621934

Almgren, S. M., & Olsson, T. (2016). Commenting, sharing and tweeting news: Measuring online news participation. *Nordicom Review, 37*(2), 67–81. http://dx.doi.org/10.1515/nor-2016-0018

Andersen, K., Shehata, A., Skovsgaard, M., & Strömbäck, J. (2024). Selective news avoidance: Consistency and temporality. *Communication Research, 0*(0). https://doi.org/10.1177/009365022312216

Anderson, B. (1983/1991). *Imagined communities: Reflections on the origin and spread of nationalism.* London & New York: Verso.

Antunovic, D., Parsons, P., & Cooke, T. R. (2018). 'Checking' and googling: Stages of news consumption among young adults. *Journalism, 19*(5), 632–648. https://doi.org/10.1177/1464884916663625

Archibald, M. M., Ambagtsheer, R. C., Casey, M. G., & Lawless, M. (2019). Using Zoom videoconferencing for qualitative data collection: Perceptions and experiences of researchers and participants. *International Journal of Qualitative Methods, 18.* https://doi.org/10.1177/1609406919874596

Armstrong, C. L., McAdams, M. J., & Cain, J. (2015). What is news? Audiences may have their own ideas. *Atlantic Journal of Communication, 23*(2), 81–98. https://doi.org/10.1080/15456870.2015.1013102

Arriagada, A., & Bishop, S. (2021). Between commerciality and authenticity: The imaginary of social media influencers in the platform economy. *Communication, Culture & Critique, 14*(4), 568–586. https://doi.org/10.1093/ccc/tcab050

Bakardjieva, M. (2005). *Internet society: The internet in everyday life.* London: Sage.

Balmas, M. (2014). When fake news becomes real: Combined exposure to multiple news sources and political attitudes of inefficacy, alienation, and cynicism. *Communication Research, 41*(3), 430–454. https://doi.org/10.1177/0093650212453600

Banjac, S. (2022). An intersectional approach to exploring audience expectations of journalism. *Digital Journalism, 10*(1), 128–147. https://doi.org/10.1080/21670811.2021.197

Barber, M. D. (1987). Constitution and the sedimentation of the social in Alfred Schutz's Theory of Typification. *Modern Schoolman, 64*(2), 111–120.

Barchas-Lichtenstein, J., Voiklis, J., Glasser, D. B., & Fraser, J. (2021). Finding relevance in the news: The scale of self-reference. *Journal of Pragmatics, 171*, 49–61. https://doi.org/10.1016/j.pragma.2020.10.001

Bausinger, H. (1984). Media, technology and daily life. *Media, Culture & Society, 6*(4), 343–351. https://doi.org/10.1177/016344378400600403

Beharrell, P., Davis, H., Edridge, J., Hewitt, J., Oddie, J., Philo, G., Walton, P., & Winston, B. (1976). *Bad news volume 1*. Routledge and Kegan Paul.

Bengtsson, S. (2006). Symbolic spaces of everyday life: Work and leisure at home. *Nordicom Review, 27*(2), 119–132.

Bengtsson, S. (2007). *Mediernas vardagsrum: Om medieanvändning och moral i Vardagslivet*. [Doctoral dissertation, Institutionen för Journalistik och masskommunikation, Göteborgs universitet.]

Bengtsson, S. (2012). Imagined user modes: Media morality in everyday life. *International Journal of Cultural Studies, 15*(2), 181–196. https://doi.org/10.1177/1367877911416883

Bengtsson, S. (2018). Sensorial organization as an ethics of space: Digital media in everyday life. *Media and Communication, 6*(2), 39–45. https://doi.org/10.17645/mac.v6i2.1337

Bengtsson, S. (2023). The relevance of digital news: Themes, scales and temporalities. *Digital Journalism*, 1–19. https://doi.org/10.1080/21670811.2022.2150254

Bengtsson, S., & Johansson, S. (2021). A phenomenology of news: Understanding news in digital culture. *Journalism, 22*(11), 2873–2889. https://doi.org/10.1177/1464884919901194

Benjamin, W. (1936/2006). The storyteller: Reflections on the works of Nikolai Leskov. In Dorothy J. Hale (Ed.), *The Novel: An Anthology of Criticism and Theory 1900–2000* (pp. 361–378). Malden, MA: Blackwell Publishing.

Bennet, A. (2005). *Culture and everyday life*. London: Sage.

Berelson, B. (1949). What missing the newspaper means. In P. Lazarsfeld & F. Stanton (Eds.), *Communications Research, 1948–1949* (pp. 111–129). New York: Harper.

Berger, P. L., & Luckmann, T. (1966). *The social construction of reality: A treatise in the sociology of knowledge*. London: Penguin Books.

Bergström, A., & Jervelycke Belfrage, M. (2018). News in social media: Incidental consumption and the role of opinion leaders. *Digital Journalism, 6*(5), 583–598. https://doi.org/10.1080/21670811.2018.1423625

Bettelheim, B. (1976/2010). *The uses of enchantment: The meaning and importance of fairy tales*. Vintage.

Bird, E. S. (1992). *For enquiring minds: A cultural study of supermarket tabloids*. Knoxville, TN: Knoxville University Press.

Bird, E. S. (1997). What a story! Understanding the audience for scandal. In J. Lull & S. Hinerman (Eds.), *Media scandals: Morality and desire in the popular cultural marketplace* (pp. 99–121). Cambridge: Polity Press.

Bird, E. S. (2000). Audience demands in a murderous market: Tabloidization in US television news. In C. Sparks & J. Tulloch (Eds.), *Tabloid tales: Global debates over media standards* (pp. 213–228). Oxford: Roman & Littlefield.

Bird, E. S. (2003). *The audience in everyday life: Living in a media world*. New York & London: Routledge.

Bird, E. S. (2010). Introduction: The anthropology of news and journalism: Why now? In E. S. Bird (Ed.), *The anthropology of news and journalism: Global perspectives* (pp. 1–20). Bloomington: Indiana University Press.

Bird, E. S. (2011). Seeking the audience for news: Response, news talk, and everyday practices. In V. Nightingale (Ed.), *The handbook of media audiences* (pp. 489–508). Malden: John Wiley & Sons.

Blöbaum, B. (2016). Key factors in the process of trust: On the analysis of trust under digital conditions. In B. Blöbaum (Ed.), *Trust and communication in a digitized world* (pp. 3–25). Dordrecht: Springer, Cham.

Boczkowski, P. J. (2021). *Abundance: On the experience of living in a world of information plenty*. New York: Oxford University Press.

Boczkowski, P. J., & Mitchelstein, E. (2013). *The news gap: When the information preferences of the media and the public diverge*. Cambridge, MA: MIT Press.

Boczkowski, P. J., Mitchelstein, E., & Matassi, M. (2018). "News comes across when I'm in a moment of leisure": Understanding the practices of incidental news consumption on social media. *New Media & Society, 20*(10), 3523–3539.

Bode, L. (2016). Political news in the news feed: Learning politics from social media. *Mass Communication and Society, 19*(24–48), 1532–7825. https://doi.org/10.1080/15205436.2015.1045149

Bolin, G. (2017). *Media generations: Experience, identity and mediatised social change*. London: Routledge.

Bolin, G., Kalmus, V., & Figueiras, R. (2023). Conducting online focus group interviews with two generations: Methodological experiences and reflections from the pandemic context. *International Journal of Qualitative Methods, 22*. https://doi.org/10.1177/16094069231182029

Bourdieu, P. (1991). *Language and symbolic power*. Cambridge, MA: Harvard University Press.

Broersma, M., & Graham, T. (2013). Twitter as a news source: How Dutch and British newspapers used tweets in their news coverage, 2007–2011. *Journalism Practice, 7*(4), 446–464. https://doi.org/10.1080/17512786.2013.802481

Broersma, M., & Peters, C. (2013). Introduction: Rethinking journalism: The structural transformation of a public good. In C. Peters & M. Broersma (Eds.), *Rethinking journalism: Trust and participation in a transformed news landscape* (pp. 1–12). London: Routledge.

Bucher, T. (2018). Programming the news: When algorithms come to matter. In T. Bucher, *If ... Then: Algorithmic power and politics* (pp. 118–148). Oxford: Oxford University Press.

Bucher, T. (2020). The right-time web: Theorizing the kairologic of algorithmic media. *New Media & Society, 22*(9), 1699–1714. https://doi.org/10.1177/146144482091356

Buckingham, D. (2000). *The making of citizens: Young people, news & politics*. London & New York: Routledge.

Buozis, M., & Creech, B. (2018). Reading news as narrative. *Journalism Studies, 19*(10), 1430–1446. https://doi.org/10.1080/1461670X.2017.1279030

Burke, P. (1978/2017). *Popular culture in early modern Europe*. Abingdon: Routledge.

Burroughs, S., Brocato, K., Hopper, P. F., & Sanders, A. (2009). Media literacy: A central component of democratic citizenship. *Educational Forum, 73*(2), 154–167.

Butsch, R. (2008) (Ed.). *Media and public spheres*. Houndmills: Palgrave Macmillan.

Campo, E. (2015). Relevance as social matrix of attention in Alfred Schutz. Societámutamentopolitica (*Sociology and the Life-World*), *12*(6), 117–148.

Cannon, D. F., & Mackay, J. B. (2017). Millennials fail to embrace civic duty to keep informed. *Newspaper Research Journal, 38*(3), 306–315. https://doi.org/10.1177/0739532917722972

Carey, J. W. (1975). A cultural approach to the study of communication. In J. W. Carey (Ed.), *Communication as culture: Essays on media and society (collected works)* (pp. 13–36). New York: Hyman/Routledge.

Casero-Ripollés, A. (2012). Más allá de los diarios: El consumo de noticias de los jóvenes en la era Digital [Beyond newspapers: News consumption among young people in the digital Era] 1–16. https://doi.org/10.3916/C39-2012-03-05

Castells, M. (2000). *The rise of the network society*, Vol 1. Oxford & Malden, MA: Blackwell Publishers.

Clark, L. S., & Marchi, R. (2017). *Young people and the future of news: Social media and the rise of connective journalism.* Cambridge: Cambridge University Press.

Cmiel, K., & Durham Peters, J. (2020). *Promiscuous knowledge: Information, image and other truth games in history.* Chicago & London: University of Chicago Press.

Collao, K. (2022). *The Kaleidoscope: Tracking young people's relationships with news.* Reuter's Institute for the Study of Journalism, University of Oxford. https://reutersinstitute.politics.ox.ac.uk/news/kaleidoscope-tracking-young-peoples-relationships-news

Conboy, M. (2002). *The press and popular culture.* London: Sage.

Costera Meijer, I. (2007). The paradox of popularity: How young people experience the news. *Journalism Studies, 8*(1), 96–116.

Costera Meijer, I. (2020). Understanding the audience turn in journalism: From quality discourse to innovation discourse as anchoring practices 1995–2020. *Journalism Studies, 21*(16), 2326–2342. https://doi.org/10.1080/1461670X.2020.1847681

Costera Meijer, I., & Groot Kormelink, T. (2015). Checking, sharing, clicking and linking: Changing patterns of news use between 2004–2014. *Digital Journalism, 3*(5), 664–679. https://doi.org/10.1080/21670811.2014.937149

Costera Meijer, I., & Groot Kormelink, T. (2020). *Changing news use: Unchanged news experiences.* London & New York: Routledge.

Couldry, N. (2004). Theorising media as practice. *Social Semiotics, 14*(2), 115–132. https://doi.org/10.1080/1035033042000238295

Couldry, N. (2005). *Media rituals: A critical approach.* London: Routledge.

Couldry, N. (2012). *Media, society, world: Social theory and digital media practice.* Cambridge: Polity.

Couldry, N., & Hepp, A. (2016). *The mediated construction of reality.* Cambridge: Polity Press.

Couldry, N., Livingstone, S., & Markham, T. (2007a). Public connection and the uncertain norms of media consumption. In K. Soper & F. Trentmann (Eds.), *Citizenship and consumption* (pp. 104–120). Basingstoke: Palgrave Macmillan.

Couldry, N., Livingstone, S., & Markham, T. (2007b). *Media consumption and public engagement: Beyond the presumption of attention.* New York: Palgrave Macmillan.

Couldry, N., Livingstone, S., & Markham, T. (2008). Connection or disconnection? Tracking the mediated public sphere in everyday life. In R. Butsch (Ed.), *Media and public spheres* (pp. 28–42). Houndmills: Palgrave Macmillan.

Curran, J., & Seaton, J. (2018). *Power without responsibility: Press, broadcasting and the Internet in Britain.* London: Routledge.

Dabbous, A., Aoun Barakat, K., & de Quero Navarro, B. (2021). Fake news detection and social media trust: A cross-cultural perspective. *Behaviour & Information Technology,* 1–20. https://doi.org/10.1080/0144929X.2021.1963475

Dahlgren, P. (2000). Media, citizenship and civic culture. In J. Curran & M. Gurevitch (Eds.), *Mass Media and Society* (pp. 310–328). London: Arnold.

Dahlgren, P. (2009). *Media and political engagement.* Cambridge: Cambridge University Press.

Dahlgren, P., & Hill, A. (2022). *Media engagement.* London: Routledge.

Dahlgren, P., & Sparks, C. (Eds.) (1991). *Communication and citizenship: Journalism and the public sphere in the new media age.* London: Routledge.

Darnton, R. (2000). An early information society: News and the media in early eighteenth-century Paris. *American Historical Review, 106*(1), 1–35.

Denisova, A. (2019). *Internet memes and society: Social, cultural, and political contexts.* London: Routledge.

Desjarlais, R., & Throop, C. J. (2011). Phenomenological approaches in anthropology. *Annual Review of Anthropology, 40*, 87–102.

Deuze, M. (2012). *Media life.* Cambridge: Polity Press.

Deuze, M., & Witschge, T. (2020). *Beyond journalism.* Cambridge: Polity Press.

DeVito, M. A. (2016). From editors to algorithms: A values-based approach to understanding story selection in the Facebook news feed. *Digital Journalism, 5*(6), 753–773. https://doi.org/10.1080/21670811.2016.1178592

Dewey, J. (1916/1923). *Democracy and education: An introduction to the philosophy of education.* New York: Macmillan.

De Zúñiga, H., Weeks, B., & Ardèvol-Abreu, A. (2017). Effects of the news-finds-me perception in communication: Social media use implications for news seeking and learning about politics. *Journal of Computer-Mediated Communication, 22*(3), 105–123.

De Zúñiga, H. G., Strauss, N., & Huber, B. (2020). The proliferation of the 'news finds me' perception across societies. *International Journal of Communication, 14*, 29.

Dimmick, J., Feaster, J. C., & Hoplamazian, G. J. (2011). News in the interstices: The niches of mobile media in space and time. *New Media & Society, 13*(1), 23–39.

Dolata, U., & Schrape, J. F. (2016). Masses, crowds, communities, movements: Collective action in the internet age. *Social Movement Studies, 15*(1), 1–18.

Edgerly, S. (2022). The head and heart of news avoidance: How attitudes about the news media relate to levels of news consumption. *Journalism, 23*(9), 1828–1845. https://doi.org/10.1177/14648849211012922

Edgerly, S., & Vraga, E. K. (2020a). That's not news: Audience perceptions of 'news-ness' and why it matters. *Mass Communication and Society, 23*(5), 730–754. https://doi.org/10.1080/15205436.2020.1729383

Edgerly, S., & Vraga, E. K. (2020b). Deciding what's news: News-ness as an audience concept for the hybrid media environment. *Journalism & Mass Communication Quarterly, 97*(2), 416–434. https://doi.org/10.1177/1077699020916808

Edgerly, S., Vraga, E. K., Bode, L., Thorson, K., & Thorson, E. (2018). New media, new relationship to participation? A closer look at youth news repertoires and political participation. *Journalism & Mass Communication Quarterly, 95*(1), 192–212. https://doi.org/10.1177/1077699017706928

Eldridge, J. (1993) (Ed.). *Getting the message: News, truth and power.* London: Routledge.

Elvestad, E., Blekesaune, A., & Aalberg, T. (2014). The polarized news audience? A longitudinal study of news-seekers and news-avoiders in Europe. *SSRN Electronic Journal.* http://dx.doi.org/10.2139/ssrn.2469713.

Enli, G., & Rosenberg, L. T. (2018). Trust in the age of social media: "Populist politicians seem more authentic". *Social Media + Society, 4*(1). https://doi.org/10.1177/2056305118764430

Enroth, H. (2023). Crisis of authority: The truth of post-truth. *International Journal of Politics, Culture, and Society, 36*(2), 179–195.

Entman, R. M. (1993). Framing: Toward clarification of a fractured paradigm. *Journal of Communication, 43*(4), 5–58. https://doi.org/10.1111/j.1460-2466.1993.tb01304.xC

Entman, R. M. (2007). Framing bias: Media in the distribution of power. *Journal of Communication, 57*(1), 163–173.

Ess, C. (2014). Selfhood, moral agency, and the good life in mediatized worlds? Perspectives from medium theory and philosophy. In K. Lundby (Ed.), *Mediatization of communication (Vol. 21, Handbook of Communication Science)* (pp. 617–640). Berlin: De Gruyter Mouton.

Fisher, C. (2016). The trouble with 'trust' in news media. *Communication Research and Practice*, *2*(4), 451–465. https://doi.org/10.1080/22041451.2016.1261251

Fletcher, R., & Park, S. (2017). The impact of trust in the news media on online news consumption and participation. *Digital Journalism*, *5*(10), 1281–1299.

Fletcher, R., & Nielsen, R. K. (2018). Are people incidentally exposed to news on social media? A comparative analysis. *New Media and Society*, *20*(7), 2450–2468.

Fraser, N. (1992). Rethinking the public sphere: A contribution to the critique of actually existing democracy. In C. Calhoun (Ed.), *Habermas and the Public Sphere* (pp. 109–142). Cambridge: MIT Press.

Galan, L., Osserman, J., Parker, T., & Taylor, M. (2019). How young people consume news and the implications for mainstream media. Reuters Institute for the Study of Journalism. Oxford: Oxford University.

Galtung, J., & Ruge, M. H. (1965). The structure of foreign news: The presentation of the Congo, Cuba and Cyprus crises in four Norwegian newspapers. *Journal of Peace Research*, *2*(1), 64–90. https://doi.org/10.1177/002234336500200104

Gans, H. (1979). *Deciding what's news.* New York: Pantheon.

Gauntlett, D., & Hill, A. (1999). *TV living: Television, culture and everyday life.* London: Routledge.

Giddens, A. (1984). *The constitution of society: Outline of a theory of structuration.* Berkeley: University of California Press.

Gillen, J., Cameron, C. A., Tapanya, S., Pinto, G., Hancock, R., Young, S., & Gamannossi, B. A. (2007). 'A day in the life': Advancing a methodology for the cultural study of development and learning in early childhood. *Early Child Development and Care*, *177*(2), 207–218. https://doi.org/10.1080/03004430500393763

Giorgi, A. (2006). Concerning variations in the application of the phenomenological method. *Humanistic Psychologist*, *34*(4), 305–319.

Giorgi, A. (2009). *The descriptive phenomenological method in psychology: A modified Husserlian approach.* Pittsburgh, PA: Duquesne University Press.

Giorgi, B. (2006). Can an empirical psychology be drawn from Husserl's phenomenology? In P. D. Ashworth & M. C. Chung (Eds.), *Phenomenology and psychological science: Historical and philosophical perspectives* (pp. 69–78). New York: Springer.

Gitlin, T. A. (1977). *"The whole world is watching": Mass media and the new left, 1965–70.* Berkeley, CA: University of California Press.

Goffman, E. (1975). *Frame analysis: The social organization of experience.* New York: Harper.

Gorski, L. C., & Thomas, F. (2021). Staying tuned or tuning out? A longitudinal analysis of news-avoiders on the micro and macro-level. *Communication Research*, 00936502211025907.

Goyanes, M., Ardèvol-Abreu, A., & Gil de Zúñiga, H. (2023). Antecedents of news avoidance: Competing effects of political interest, news overload, trust in news media, and 'news finds me' perception. *Digital Journalism*, *11*(1), 1–18.

Groot Kormelink, T., & Costera Meijer, I. C. (2018). What clicks actually mean: Exploring digital news user practices. *Journalism*, *19*(5), 668–683. https://doi.org/10.1177/1464884916688290

Groot Kormelink, T., & Costera Meijer, I. (2019). Material and sensory dimensions of everyday news use. *Media, Culture & Society*, *41*(5), 637–653. https://doi.org/10.1177/0163443718810910

Groot Kormelink, T., & Costera Meijer, I. (2020). A user perspective on time spent: Temporal experiences of everyday news use. *Journalism Studies*, *21*(2), 271–286. https://doi.org/10.1080/1461670X.2019.1639538

Habermas, J. (1989). *The structural transformation of the public sphere: An inquiry into a category of bourgeois society.* Cambridge: Polity Press.

Hagen, I. (1992). *News viewing ideals and everyday practices: The ambivalence of watching 'Dagsrevyen'.* Bergen: Department of Mass Communication.

Hagen, I. (1994). The ambivalences of TV news viewing: Between ideals and everyday practices. *European Journal of Communication, 9*(2), 193–220.

Haider, J., & Sundin, O. (2022). *Paradoxes of media and information literacy: The crisis of information.* London: Routledge.

Hall, S., Critcher, C., Jefferson, T., Clarke, J., & Roberts, B. (1978). *Policing the crisis: Mugging, the state, and law and order.* London: Macmillan.

Hanitzsch, T., Van Dalen, A., & Steindl, N. (2018). Caught in the nexus: A comparative and longitudinal analysis of public trust in the press. *International Journal of Press/Politics, 23*(1), 3–23. https://doi.org/10.1177/1940161217740695

Hardin, R. (2002). *Trust and trustworthiness.* New York: Russell Sage Foundation.

Heidegger, M. (1996). *Being and time: A translation of Sein und Zeit.* Albany, NY: SUNY Press.

Heikkilä, H., & Ahva, L. (2015). The relevance of journalism: Studying news audiences in a digital era. *Journalism Practice, 9*(1), 50–64.

Heikkilä, H., Kunelius, R., & Ahva, L. (2010). From credibility to relevance: Towards a sociology of journalism's 'added value'. *Journalism Practice, 4*(3), 274–284.

Hendrickx, J. (2024). 'Normal news is boring': How young adults encounter and experience news on Instagram and TikTok. *new media & society,* 14614448241255955.

Hepp, A. (2020). *Deep mediatization.* London: Routledge.

Hermes, J. (1995). *Reading women's magazines.* Cambridge: Polity Press.

Hermida, A. (2010). Twittering the news: The emergence of ambient journalism. *Journalism Practice, 4*(3), 297–308. https://doi.org/10.1080/17512781003640703

Hermida, A., Fletcher, F., Korell, D., & Logan, D. (2012). Share, like, recommend: Decoding the social media news consumer. *Journalism Studies, 13*(5–6), 815–824. https://doi.org/10.1080/1461670X.2012.664430

Hermida, A., & Young, M. L. (2019). *Data journalism and the regeneration of news.* London: Routledge.

Highfield, T. (2016). *Social media and everyday politics.* Cambridge: Polity Press.

Highmore, B. (2001). *Everyday life and cultural theory: An introduction.* London: Routledge.

Hill, A. (2007). Restyling factual TV: Audiences and news, documentary and reality genres. London and New York: Routledge.

Hobson, D. (1982). *Crossroads: The drama of a soap opera.* London: Methuen.

Holt, K., Strömbäck, J., Shehata, A., & Ljungberg, E. (2013). Age and the effects of news media attention and social media use on political interest and participation: Do social media function as a leveller? *European Journal of Communication, 28*(1), 5–18. https://doi.org/10.1177/026732311246536

Horowitz, M., Ojala, M., Matikainen, J., & Jääsaari, J. (2021). The multidimensionality of trust: Assessing Finnish audiences' views on the trustworthiness of digital news. *Global Perspectives, 2*(1), 19054.

Hovden, J. F., & Moe, H. (2017). A sociocultural approach to study public connection across and beyond media: The example of Norway. *Convergence, 23*(4), 391–408. https://doi.org/10.1177/13548565177003

Husserl, E. (1900–1901/2001). *Logical investigations I–II* (trans. J. N. Findlay). London: Routledge.

Husserl, E. (1931). *Ideas: General introduction to phenomenology, Vol. 1* (trans. W. R. R. Gibson). London: George Allen & Unwin.

Husserl, E. (1936/1970). *The crisis of European sciences and transcendental phenomenology: An introduction to phenomenological philosophy* (trans. D. Carr). Evanstone, IL: Northwestern University Press.

Husserl, E. (1999). *The essential Husserl: Basic writings in transcendental phenomenology.* Bloomington, IN: Indiana University Press.

Hutchison, P. J. (2020). Media rituals and memory: Exploring the historical phenomenology of American local television. *Journal of Communication Inquiry, 45*(3), 225–243. https://doi.org/10.1177/019685992097712

Ihde, D. (1993). *Postphenomenology: Essays in the postmodern context.* Evanston, IL: Northwestern University Press.

Ihde, D. (2003). *Postphenomenology – again.* Aarhus: Department of Information & Media Studies.

Internetstiftelsen (2023). *Svenskarna och internet 2023.* https://svenskarnaochinternet.se/rapporter/svenskarna-och-internet-2023/

Jackob, N. G. E. (2010). No alternatives? The relationship between perceived media dependency, use of alternative information sources, and general trust in mass media. *International Journal of Communication, 4,* 589–606.

Jakobsson, P., & Stiernstedt, F. (2023). Trust and the media: Arguments for the (irr)elevance of a concept. *Journalism Studies, 24*(4), 479–495. https://doi.org/10.1525/gp.2021.19054

Jansson, A., & Lindell, J. (2015). News media consumption in the transmedia age. *Journalism Studies, 16*(1), 79–96.

Ji, Q., Ha, L., & Sypher, U. (2014). The role of news media use and demographic characteristics in the possibility of information overload prediction. *International Journal of Communication, 8,* 16.

Johansson, S. (2007). *Reading tabloids: Tabloid newspapers and their readers.* Huddinge: Södertörn Academic Series.

Johansson, S. (2008). Gossip, sport and pretty girls: What does 'trivial' journalism mean to tabloid newspaper readers? *Journalism Practice, 2*(3), 402–413.

Johansson, S. (2015). Celebrity culture and audiences: A Swedish case study. *Celebrity Studies, 6*(1), 54–68.

Johansson, S. (2020a). The tabloid press: Tales of controversy, community and public life. In M. Conboy & A. Bingham (Eds.), *The Edinburgh history of the British and Irish press: Competition and disruption, 1900–2017* (pp. 517–537). Edinburgh: Edinburgh University Press.

Johansson, S. (2020b). Tabloid journalism and tabloidization. *Oxford Research Encyclopaedia of Communication.* February 28, 1–23. https://doi.org/10.1093/acrefore/9780190228613.013.877

Jones, D. A. (2004). Why Americans don't trust the media: A preliminary analysis. *Harvard International Journal of Press/Politics, 9*(2), 60–75.

Jordheim, H., & Ytreberg, E. (2021). After supersynchronisation: How media synchronise the social. *Time & Society, 30*(3), 402–422.

Kalogeropoulos, A., Suiter, J., Udris, L., & Eisenegger, M. (2019). News media trust and news consumption: Factors related to trust in news in 35 countries. *International Journal of Communication, 13*(22).

Kammer, A., Boeck, M., Hansen, J. V., & Hauschildt, L. J. H. (2015). The free-to-fee transition: Audiences' attitudes toward paying for online news. *Journal of Media Business Studies, 12*(2), 107–120. https://doi.org/10.1080/16522354.2015.1053345

Karlsen, R., Beyer, A., & Steen-Johnsen, K. (2020). Do high-choice media environments facilitate news avoidance? A longitudinal study 1997–2016. *Journal of Broadcasting & Electronic Media, 64*(5), 794–814. https://doi.org/10.1080/08838151.2020.1835428

Karlsson, M., Bergström, A., Clerwall, C., & Fast, K. (2015). Participatory journalism – The (r)evolution that wasn't: Content and user behavior in Sweden 2007–2013. *Journal of Computer-Mediated Communication, 20*(3), 295–311. https://doi.org/10.1111/jcc4.12115

Katz, D. (1989). *The world of touch* (trans. L. D. Kruger). Hillsdale, NJ: Lawrence Erlbaum Associates.

Kaun, A. (2012). *Civic experiences and public connection: Media and young people in Estonia.* [PhD thesis, Örebro University.]

Kaun, A. (2017). "Our time to act has come": desynchronization, social media time and protest movements. *Media, Culture & Society, 39*(4), 469–486.

Kaun, A., & Stiernstedt, F. (2014). Facebook time: Technological and institutional affordances for media memories. *New Media & Society, 16*(7), 1154–1168.

Keightley, E., & Downey, J. (2018). The intermediate time of news consumption. *Journalism, 19*(1), 93–110. https://doi.org/10.1177/1464884916689155

Kiousis, S. (2001). Public trust or mistrust? Perceptions of media credibility in the information age. *Mass Communication & Society, 4*, 381–403.

Kitzinger, J., & Barbour, R. (Eds.) (1999). *Developing focus group research: Politics, theory and practice.* London: Sage.

Knudsen, E., Dahlberg, S., Iversen, M. H., Johannesson, M. P., & Nygaard, S. (2021). How the public understands news media trust: An open-ended approach. *Journalism, 23*(11). https://doi.org/10.1177/14648849211005892

Kruikemeier, S., & Shehata, A. (2017). News media use and political engagement among adolescents: An analysis of virtuous circles using panel data. *Political Communication, 34*(2), 221–242. https://doi.org/10.1080/10584609.2016.1174760

Ksiazek, T. B., Malthouse, E. C., & Webster, J. G. (2010). News-seekers and avoiders: Exploring patterns of total news consumption across media and the relationship to civic participation. *Journal of Broadcasting & Electronic Media, 54*(4), 551–568. https://doi.org/10.1080/08838151.2010.519808

Langeveld, M. J. (1972). *Capita uit de algemene methodologie der opvoedingwetenshap [Capital from the general methodology of pedagogical science]*. Groeningen: Wolters-Nordhoff.

Larsen, B. S. (2000). Radio as ritual. *Nordicom Review, 21*(2), 259–274.

Larsson, A. O. (2018). I shared the news today, oh boy. *Journalism Studies, 19*(1), 43–61. https://doi.org/10.1080/1461670X.2016.1154797

Lash, S., & Urry, J. (1994). *Economies of signs and space.* London, Thousand Oaks, CA & New Delhi: Sage.

Lee, A. M., & Chyi, H. I. (2014). When newsworthy is not noteworthy: Examining the value of news from the audience's perspective. *Journalism studies, 15*(6), 807–820.

Lee, T.-T. (2010). Why they don't trust the media: An examination of factors predicting trust. *American Behavioral Scientist, 54*(1), 8–21. https://doi.org/10.1177/0002764210376308

Lefebvre, H. (1991). *Critique of everyday life.* Vol. 1. London: Verso.

Lefebvre, H. (2013). *Rhythmanalysis: Space, time and everyday life.* Bloomsbury Publishing.

Lindell, J. (2018). Distinction recapped: Digital news repertoires in the class structure. *New Media & Society, 20*(8), 3029–3049. https://doi.org/10.1177/1461444817739622

Lindell, J., & Mikkelsen Båge, E. (2023). Disconnecting from digital news: News avoidance and the ignored role of social class. *Journalism, 24*(9), 1980–1997.

https://doi.org/10.1177/14648849221085389

Livio, O., & Cohen, J. (2018). "Fool me once, shame on you": Direct personal experience and media trust. *Journalism, 19*(5), 684–698. https://doi.org/10.1177/146488491667133

Luhmann, N. (2017). *Trust and power.* Cambridge: Polity Press.

Lull, J. (1990). *Inside family viewing: Ethnographic research on television audiences.* London: Routledge.

Madianou, M. (2013). Living with news: Ethnography and news consumption. In S. Allan (Ed.), *The Routledge companion to news and journalism studies* (pp. 428–438). London: Routledge.

Marchi, R. (2012). With Facebook, blogs, and fake news, teens reject journalistic 'objectivity'. *Journal of Communication Inquiry, 36*(3), 246–262. https://doi.org/10.1177/019685991245870

Markham, T. (2023) (2nd ed.). *Media and everyday life.* London, New York & Dublin: Bloomsbury Publishing.

Martin, V. B. (2008). Attending the news: A grounded theory about a daily regimen. *Journalism, 9*(1), 76–94.

Matassi, M. & Boczkowski, P. J. (2023). *To know is to compare: Studying social media across nations, media and platforms.* Cambridge: MIT Press.

Matthes, J., Nanz, A., Stubenvoll, M., & Heiss, R. (2020). Processing news on social media. The political incidental news exposure model (PINE). *Journalism, 21*(8), 1031–1048. https://doi.org/10.1177/1464884920915371

Mattingly, C., & Throop, J. (2018). The anthropology of ethics and morality. *Annual Review of Anthropology, 47,* 475–492.

May, T. (2001). *Social research: Issues, methods and process* (3rd ed.). Buckingham: Open University Press.

McCombs, M., & Poindexter, P. (1983). The duty to keep informed: News exposure and civic obligation. *Journal of Communication, 33*(2), 89–96. https://doi.org/10.1111/j.1460-2466.1983.tb02391.x

McLuhan, M. (1964/1994). *Understanding media: The extensions of man.* MIT press.

McNair, B. (2013). Trust, truth and objectivity: Sustaining quality journalism in the era of the content-generating user. In C. Peters & M. Broersma (Eds.), *Rethinking journalism: Trust and participation in a transformed news landscape* (pp. 75–88). London: Routledge.

Merleau-Ponty, M. (1962). *Phenomenology of perception* [*Phénoménologie de la perception*]. London: Routledge & Kegan Paul.

Meyrowitz, J. (1986). *No sense of place: The impact of electronic media on social behavior.* Oxford: Oxford University Press.

Mihalidis, P. (2012). *News literacy: Global perspectives for the newsroom and the classroom.* New York: Peter Lang.

Milner, R. M. (2018). *The world made meme: Public conversations and participatory media.* Cambridge: MIT Press.

Miltner, K. M. (2018). Internet memes. In J. Burgess, A. Marwick, & T. Poell (Eds.), *The SAGE handbook of social media* (pp. 412–428). London: Sage.

Misztal, B. A. (1996). *Trust in modern societies: The search for the bases of social order.* Cambridge: Polity Press.

Mitchelstein, E., & Boczkowski, P. J. (2010). Online news consumption research: An assessment of past work and an agenda for the future. *New Media & Society, 12*(7), 1085–1102. https://doi.org/10.1177/1461444809350193

Moe, H. (2020). Distributed readiness citizenship: A realistic, normative concept for citizens' public connection. *Communication Theory, 30*(2), 205–225. https://doi.org/10.1093/ct/qtz016

Moe, H., & Ytre-Arne, B. (2022). The democratic significance of everyday news use: Using diaries to understand public connection over time and beyond journalism. *Digital Journalism, 10*(1), 43 – 61.

Möller, J. (2021). Filter bubbles and digital echo chambers. In H. Tumber & S. Waisbord (Eds.), *The Routledge companion to media disinformation and populism* (pp. 92 – 100). Oxon & New York: Routledge.

Molyneux, L. (2017). Mobile news consumption: A habit of snacking. *Digital Journalism, 6*(5), 634 – 650. https://doi.org/10.1080/21670811.2017.1334567

Moores, S. (1988). "The box on the dresser": Memories of early radio and everyday life. *Media, Culture & Society, 10*(1), 23 – 40. https://doi.org/10.1177/016344388010001003

Moores, S. (1993). *Interpreting audiences: The ethnography of media consumption.* Vol. 8. London: Sage.

Moores, S. (2000). *Media and everyday life in modern society.* Edinburgh: Edinburgh University Press.

Moores, S. (2011). That familiarity with the world born of habit: A phenomenological approach to the study of media uses in daily living. *Interactions: Studies in Communication & Culture, 1*(3), 301 – 312.

Moores, S. (2012). *Media, place and mobility.* Basingstoke: Palgrave Macmillan.

Morley, D. (1980). *The Nationwide audience.* London: British Film Institute.

Morley, D. (1986). *Family television: Cultural power and domestic leisure.* London: Comedia.

Morley, J. (2019). Phenomenology in nursing studies: New perspectives – commentary. *International Journal of Nursing Studies,* (93), 163 – 167.

Muzzetto, L. (2006). *Il soggetto e il sociale: Alfred Schütz e il mondo taken for granted.* Milan: FrancoAngeli.

Nasu, H. (2008). A continuing dialogue with Alfred Schutz. *Human Studies, 31*(2), 87 – 105.

Negt, O., & Kluge, A. (1972 [German]/1993). *Public sphere and experience: Toward an analysis of the experience of the bourgeois and proletarian public sphere.* Minnesota: University of Minnesota Press.

Nelson, J. L. (1986). Television and its audiences as dimensions of being: Critical theory and phenomenology. *Human Studies, 9*(1), 55 – 69. https://doi.org/10.1007/BF00142909

Nelson, J. L. (1990). The dislocation of time: A phenomenology of television reruns. *Quarterly Review of Film and Video, 12*(3), 79 – 92. https://doi.org/10.1080/10509209009361354

Newman, N., Fletcher, R., Kalogeropoulos, A., Levy, D. A. L., & Nielsen, R. K. (2018). *Reuters Institute digital news report 2018.* https://ssrn.com/abstract=32453551

Newman, N., with Fletcher, R., Eddy, K., Robertson, C. T., & Nielsen, R. K. (2023). *Reuters Institute digital news report 2023.* https://reutersinstitute.politics.ox.ac.uk/sites/default/files/2023-06/Digital_News_Report_2023.pdf

Oeldorf-Hirsch, A., & Srinivasan, P. (2022). An unavoidable convenience: How post-millennials engage with the news that finds them on social and mobile media. *Journalism, 23*(9), 1939 – 1954. https://doi.org/10.1177/1464884921990251

Ognyanova, K. (2019). The social context of media trust: A network influence model. *Journal of Communication, 69*(5), 539 – 562. https://doi.org/10.1093/joc/jqz031

Ojala, M., & Ripatti-Torniainen, L. (2023). Where is the public of 'networked publics'? A critical analysis of the theoretical limitations of online publics research. *European Journal of Communication, 39*(2). https://doi.org/10.1177/02673231231210207

Ong, W (1982/2002). *Orality and Literacy: The technologization of the word.* London: Routledge.

Örnebring, H. (2016). *Newsworkers: A comparative European perspective.* London: Bloomsbury Academic.

Örnebring, H., & Hellekant Rowe, E. (2022). The media day, revisited: Rhythm, place and hyperlocal information environments. *Digital Journalism, 10*(1), 23 – 42. https://doi.org/10.1080/21670811.2021.1884988

Örnebring, H., & Karlsson, M. (2022). *Journalistic autonomy: The genealogy of a Concept.* Columbia, MO: University of Missouri Press.

Palmer, R., & Toff, B. (2020). What does it take to sustain a news habit? The role of civic duty norms and a connection to a 'news community' among news avoiders in the UK and Spain. *International Journal of Communication, 14*, 1634 – 1653.

Papacharissi, Z. (2015). Toward new journalism(s): Affective news, hybridity and liminal spaces. *Journalism Studies, 16*(1), 27 – 40. https://doi.org/10.1080/1461670X.2014.890328

Papathanassopoulos, S., Coen, S., Curran, J. P., Aalberg, T., Rowe, D., Jones, P. K., Rojas, H., & Tiffen, R. (2013). Online threat but television still dominant: A comparative study of 11 nations' news consumption. *Journalism Practice, 7*(6), 690 – 704. https://doi.org/10.1080/17512786.2012.761324

Pariser, E. (2011). *The filter bubble: How the new personalized web is changing what we read and how we think.* London: Penguin Press.

Park, C. S. (2019). Does too much news on social media discourage news seeking? Mediating role of news efficacy between perceived news overload and news avoidance on social media. *Social Media + Society, 5*(3), 2056305119872956.

Park, C. S., & Kaye, B. K. (2020). What's this? Incidental exposure to news on social media, news-finds-me perception, news efficacy, and news consumption. *Mass Communication & Society, 23*(2), 157 – 180. https://doi.org/10.1080/15205436.2019.1702216

Pentina, I., & Tarafdar, M. (2014). From 'information' to 'knowing': Exploring the role of social media in contemporary news consumption. *Computers in Human Behavior, 35*, 211 – 223. https://doi.org/10.1016/j.chb.2014.02.045

Peters, C. (2012). Journalism to go: The changing spaces of news consumption. *Journalism Studies, 13*(5 – 6), 695 – 705. https://doi.org/10.1080/1461670X.2012.662405

Peters, C., & Schrøder, K. C. (2018). Beyond the here and now of news audiences: A process-based framework for investigating news repertoires. *Journal of Communication, 68*(6), 1079 – 1103. https://doi.org/10.1093/joc/jqy060

Peters, C., Schrøder, K. C., Lehaff, J., & Vulpius, J. (2022). News as they know it: Young adults' information repertoires in the digital media landscape. *Digital Journalism, 10*(1), 62 – 86. https://doi.org/10.1080/21670811.2021.1885986

Pettegree, A. (2014). *The invention of news: How the world came to know about itself.* New Haven, CT: Yale University Press.

Pettitt, T. (2013). Media dynamics and the lessons of history: the "Gutenberg Parenthesis" as Restoration Topos. In J. Hartley, J. Burgess & A. Bruns (Eds.), *A companion to new media dynamics* (pp. 53 – 72). John Wiley and Sons Australia.

Phillips, A. (2012). Sociability, speed and quality in the changing news environment. *Journalism Practice, 6*(5 – 6), 669 – 679. https://doi.org/10.1080/17512786.2012.689476

Picone, I. (2011). Produsage as a form of self-publication: A qualitative study of casual news produsage. *New Review of Hypermedia and Multimedia, 17*(1), 99 – 120. https://doi.org/10.1080/13614568.2011.552643

Picone, I., Courtois, C., & Paulussen, S. (2015). When news is everywhere: Understanding participation, cross-mediality and mobility in journalism from a radical user perspective. *Journalism Practice, 9*(1), 35 – 49.

Pink, S. (2011). Multimodality, multisensoriality and ethnographic knowing: Social semiotics and the phenomenology of perception. *Qualitative Research, 11*(3), 216 – 276.

Pink, S. (2012). *Situating everyday life: Practices and places.* London: Sage.

Pink, S., & Leder Mackley, K. (2013). Saturated and situated: Expanding the meanings of media in the routines of everyday life. *Media, Culture & Society, 35*(6), 677 – 691. https://doi.org/10.1177/0163443713491298

Prior, M. (2007). *Post-broadcast democracy: How media choice increases inequality in political involvement and polarizes elections.* New York: Cambridge University Press.

Radway, J. A. (1984/2009). *Reading the romance: Women, patriarchy, and popular literature.* North Carolina: University of North Carolina Press.

Rauch, J. (2020). *Resisting the news: Engaged audiences, alternative media, and popular critique of journalism.* New York: Routledge.

Reinemann, C., Stanyer, J., Scherr, S., & Legnante, G. (2012). Hard and soft news: A review of concepts, operationalizations and key findings. *Journalism, 13*(2), 221 – 239. https://doi.org/10.1177/1464884911427803

Robertson, C. T. (2023). Defining news from an audience perspective at a time of crisis in the United States. *Journalism Practice, 17*(2), 374 – 390. https://doi.org/10.1080/17512786.2021.1919178

Scannell, P. (1995). For a phenomenology of radio and television. *Journal of Communication, 45*(3), 4 – 19. https://doi.org/10.1111/j.1460-2466.1995.tb00741.x

Scannell, P. (1996). *Radio, television, and modern life: A phenomenological approach.* Chichester: John Wiley & Sons.

Scannell, P. (2014). *Television and the meaning of 'live': An enquiry into the human situation.* Cambridge: Polity Press.

Schmitt, J. B., Debbelt, C. A., & Schneider, F. M. (2018). Too much information? Predictors of information overload in the context of online news exposure. *Information, Communication & Society, 21*(8), 1151 – 1167.

Schrøder, K. C. (2015). News media old and new: Fluctuating audiences, news repertoires and locations of consumption. *Journalism Studies, 16*(1), 60 – 78. https://doi.org/10.1080/1461670X.2014.890332

Schrøder, K. C. (2019). What do news readers really want to read about? How relevance works for news audiences. Digital News Report, Reuters Institute for the Study of Journalism. https://doi.org/10.60625/risj-n12y-az27

Schrøder, K. C., & Larsen, B. S. (2010). The shifting cross-media news landscape: Challenges for news producers. *Journalism Studies, 11*(4), 524 – 534.

Schudson, M. (1978). *Discovering the news: A social history of American newspapers.* New York: Basic Books.

Schudson, M. (1998). *The good citizen: A history of American civic life.* New York: Free Press.

Schudson, M. (2001). The objectivity norm in American journalism. *Journalism, 2*(2), 149 – 170. https://doi.org/10.1177/1464884901002002

Schudson, M. (2003). *Sociology of news.* New York: W. W. Norton.

Schutz, A. (1953). Common-sense and scientific interpretation of human action. *Philosophy and Phenomenological Research, 14*(1), 1 – 38.

Schutz, A. (1967). *The phenomenology of the social world.* Evanston, IL: Northwestern University Press.

Schutz, A. (1970). Reflections on the problem of relevance. In A. Schutz & L. Embree (Eds.), *Collected Papers V: Phenomenology and the Social Sciences* (pp. 93 – 199). Dordrecht: Springer Netherlands.

Schutz, A., & Luckmann, T. (1973). *The structures of the life-world* (Vol. 1). Evanston, IL: Northwestern University Press.

Seale, C. (1999). *The quality of qualitative research.* London & Thousand Oaks, CA: Sage.

Shehata, A., & Strömbäck, J. (2021). Learning political news from social media: Network media logic and current affairs news learning in a high-choice media environment. *Communication Research, 48*(1), 125–147. https://doi.org/10.1177/0093650217749354

Sheringham, M. (2006). *Everyday life: Theories and practices from surrealism to the present.* Oxford: Oxford University Press.

Shibutani, T. (1966). *Improvised news: A sociological study of rumor.* Indianapolis, IN: Bobbs Merrill.

Shifman, L. (2014). *Memes in digital culture.* Cambridge: MIT Press.

Shoemaker, P. J. (2006). News and newsworthiness: A commentary. *Communications, 31,* 105–111.

Shoemaker, P. J., & Cohen, A. A. (2006). *News around the world: Practicioners, content and the public.* Oxford: Routledge.

Silverstone, R. (1994). *Television and everyday life.* London: Routledge.

Simon, F. M. (2022). Uneasy bedfellows: AI in the news, platform companies and the issue of journalistic autonomy. *Digital Journalism, 10*(10), 1832–1854. https://doi.org/10.1080/21670811.2022.2063150

Skovsgaard, M., & Andersen, K. (2020). Conceptualizing news avoidance: Towards a shared understanding of different causes and potential solutions. *Journalism Studies, 21*(4), 459–476. https://doi.org/10.1080/1461670x.2019.1686410

Sperber, D., & Wilson, D. (1986). *Relevance: Communication and cognition.* Vol. 142. Cambridge, MA: Harvard University Press.

Stald, G. (2023). Mobile democracy: Changing conditions for young Danes' democratic information and participation. *Journalism and Media, 4*(1), 272–288.

Sterrett, D., Malato, D., Benz, J., Kantor, L., Tompson, T., Rosenstiel, T., & Loker, K. (2019). Who shared It? Deciding what news to trust on social media. *Digital Journalism, 7*(6), 783–801. https://doi.org/10.1080/21670811.2019.1623702

Stiernstedt, F. (2021). The voices we trust: Public trust in news and information about Covid-19 on Swedish radio. *Radio Journal: International Studies in Broadcast & Audio Media, 19*(2), 233–251.

Storey, J. (2014). *From popular culture to everyday life.* Oxon: Routledge.

Strauß, N., Huber, B., & Gil de Zúñiga, H. (2021). Structural influences on the news finds me perception: Why people believe they don't have to actively seek news anymore. *Social Media + Society, 7*(2), 1–21. https://doi.org/10.1177/20563051211024966

Strömbäck, J., Djerf-Pierre, M., & Shehata, A. (2013). The dynamics of political interest and news media consumption: A longitudinal perspective. *International Journal of Public Opinion Research, 25*(4), 415–435. https://doi.org/10.1093/ijpor/eds018

Strömbäck, J., Tsfati, Y., Boomgaarden, H., Damstra, A., Lindgren, E., Vliegenthart, R., & Lindholm, T. (2020). News media trust and its impact on media use: Toward a framework for future research. *Annals of the International Communication Association, 44*(2), 139–156. https://doi.org/10.1080/23808985.2020.1755338

Stubenvoll, M., Heiss, R., & Matthes, J. (2021). Media trust under threat: Antecedents and consequences of misinformation perceptions on social media. *International Journal of Communication, 15,* 2765–2786.

Sveningsson, M. (2015). "It's only a pastime, really": Young people's experiences of social media as a source of news about public affairs. *Social Media & Society, 1*(2), 1–11. https://doi.org/10.1177/2056305115604855

Swart, J., & Broersma, M. (2022). The trust gap: Young people's tactics for assessing the reliability of political news. *International Journal of Press/Politics, 27*(2), 396–416.

Swart, J., & Broersma, M. (2023). What feels like news? Young people's perceptions of news on Instagram. *Journalism, 0*(0). https://doi.org/10.1177/14648849231212737

Swart, J., Groot Kormelink, T., Costera Meijer, I., & Broersma, M. (2022). Advancing a radical audience turn in journalism: Fundamental dilemmas for journalism studies. *Digital Journalism, 10*(1), 8–22. https://doi.org/10.1080/21670811.2021.2024764Swart, J., Peters, C., & Broersma, M. (2016). Navigating cross-media news use: Media repertoires and the value of news in everyday life. *Journalism Studies, 18*(11),1343–1362. https://doi.org/10.1080/1461670X.2015.1129285

Swart, J., Peters, C., & Broersma, M. (2017a). The ongoing relevance of local journalism and public broadcasters: Motivations for news repertoires in the Netherlands. *Participations: Journal of Audience & Reception Studies, 14*(2), 268–282.

Swart, J., Peters, C., & Broersma, M. (2017b). Repositioning news and public connection in everyday life: A user-oriented perspective on inclusiveness, engagement, relevance, and constructiveness. *Media, Culture & Society, 39*(6), 902–918. https://doi.org/10.1177/0163443716679034

Swart, J., Peters, C., & Broersma, M. (2017c). Navigating cross-media news use. *Journalism Studies, 18*(11), 1343–1362. https://doi.org/10.1080/1461670X.2015.1129285

Swart, J., Peters, C., & Broersma, M. (2018). Shedding light on the dark social: The connective role of news and journalism in social media communities. *New Media & Society, 20*(11), 4329–4345. https://doi.org/10.1177/1461444818772063

Syvertsen, T. (2020). *Digital detox: The politics of disconnecting.* Bingley: Emerald Group

Syvertsen, T., & Enli, G. (2020). Digital detox: Media resistance and the promise of authenticity. *Convergence, 26*(5–6), 1269–1283.

Sztompka, P. (1999) *Trust: A sociologial theory.* Cambridge: Cambridge University Press. Publishing.

Thorsen, E., & Allen, S. (Eds.) (2014). *Citizen journalism: Global perspectives.* New York: Peter Lang.

Thurman, N., Moeller, J., Helberger, N., & Trilling, D. (2019). My friends, editors, algorithms, and I: Examining audience attitudes to news selection. *Digital Journalism, 7*(4), 447–469. https://doi.org/10.1080/21670811.2018.1493936

Toff, B., Badrinathan, S., Mont'Alverne, C., Ross Arguedas, A., Fletcher, R., & Kleis Nielsen, R. (2020). *What we think we know and what we want to know: Perspectives on trust in news in a changing world.* Oxford: Reuters Institute for the Study of Journalism.

Toff, B., & Palmer, R. (2019). Explaining the gender gap in news avoidance: 'News-is-for-men' perceptions and the burdens of caretaking. *Journalism Studies, 20*(11), 1563–1579.

Toff, B., Palmer, R., & Kleis Nielsen, R. (2023). *Avoiding the news: Reluctant audiences for journalism.* Columbia, OH: Columbia University Press.

Tsfati, Y., & Ariely, G. (2014). Individual and contextual correlates of trust in media across 44 countries. *Communication Research, 41*, 760–782.

Tuchman, G. (1976). Telling stories. *Journal of Communication, 26*(4), 93–97. https://doi.org/10.1111/j.1460-2466.1976.tb01942.x

Tuchman, G. (1978). *Making news: A study in the construction of reality.* New York: Peter Lang.

Tudor, M. (2018). *Desire lines: Towards a queer digital media phenomenology.* [Doctoral dissertation, Södertörn University.]

Tumber, H., & Waisbord, S. (Eds.) (2021). *The Routledge companion to media disinformation and populism.* London & New York: Routledge.

Turcotte, J., York, C., Irving, J., Scholl, R. M., & Pingree, R. J. (2015). News recommendations from social media opinion leaders: Effects on media trust and information seeking. *Journal of Computer-Mediated Communication, 20*(5), 520–535.

Turner, V. (1966). *The ritual process: Structure and anti-structure.* Ithaca, NY: Cornell University Press.

Van Damme, K., Courtois, C., Verbrugge, K., & De Marez, L. (2015). What's APPening to news? A mixed-method audience-centred study on mobile news consumption. *Mobile Media & Communication, 3*(2), 196–213. https://doi.org/10.1177/2050157914557691

Van Damme, K., Martens, M., Van Leuven, S., Abeele, M. V., & De Marez, L. (2020). Mapping the mobile DNA of news. Understanding incidental and serendipitous mobile news consumption. In A. Duffy, R. Ling, N. Kim, E. Tandoc Jr. & O. Westlund (Eds.), *Mobile news: Journalism's shift from fixed to fluid* (pp. 49–68). New York & Oxon: Routledge.

Van Dijck, J. (2013). *The culture of connectivity: A critical history of social media.* Oxford: Oxford University Press.

Van Dijck, J., Poell, T., & de Waal, M. (2018). *The platform society.* Oxford: Oxford University Press.

Van Manen, M. (2016). *Phenomenology of practice: Meaning-giving methods in phenomenological research and writing.* New York: Routledge.

Van Manen, M. (2019). Rebuttal: Doing phenomenology on the Things. *Qualitative Health Research, 29*(6), 908–925. https://doi.org/10.1177/1049732319827293

Villi, M., Aharoni, T., Tenenboim-Weinblatt, K., Boczkowski, P. J., Hayashi, K., Mitchelstein, E., & Kligler-Vilenchik, N. (2022). Taking a break from news: A five-nation study of news avoidance in the digital era. *Digital Journalism, 10*(1), 148–164. https://doi.org/10.1080/21670811.2021.1904266

Vulpius, J., Lehaff, J., Schrøder, K. C., & Peters, C. (2023). Exploring changing news repertoires: Towards a typology. *Journalism, 24*(1), 78–100. https://doi.org/10.1177/14648849211047384

Vulpius, J. (2023). "We need to think about their real needs": Examining the auxiliary work of audience-oriented intralopers in news organizations. *Digital Journalism,* 1–20. https://doi.org/10.1080/21670811.2023.2288245

Wagner, M. C., & Boczkowski, P. J. (2019). The reception of fake news: The interpretations and practices that shape the consumption of perceived misinformation. *Digital Journalism, 7*(7), 870–885.

Wahl-Jorgensen, K. (2021). The affordances of interview research on Zoom: New intimacies and active listening. *Communication, Culture & Critique, 14*(2), 373–376. https://doi.org/10.1093/ccc/tcab015

Wasserman, H. (2010). *Tabloid journalism in South Africa: True story!* Indiana, IN: Indiana University Press.

Weibull, L. (1983). *Tidningsläsning i Sverige=[Newspaper readership in Sweden: tidningsinnehav, tidningsval, läsvanor].* Göteborg: Göteborgs Universitet.

Westlund, O., & Bjur, J. (2013). Mobile news life of the young. In K. M. Cumiskey & L. Hjorth (Eds.), *Mobile Media Practices, Presence and Politics* (pp. 180–197). Routledge.

Westlund, O., & Lewis, S. C. (2014). Agents of media innovations: Actors, actants, and audiences. *Journal of Media Innovations, 1*(2), 10–35.

Wiggins, B. E. (2019). *The discursive power of memes in digital culture: Ideology, semiotics, and intertextuality.* London & New York: Routledge.

Williams, R. (1962). *Communications.* London: Penguin.

Wilson, D., & Sperber, D. (2006). Relevance theory. In L. R. Horn & G. Ward (Eds.), *Handbook of pragmatics* (pp. 607–632). Oxford: Blackwell.

Ytre-Arne, B. (2023). *Media use in digital everyday life.* Bingley: Emerald Publishing.

Zahavi, D. (2019). Getting it quite wrong: Van Manen and Smith on phenomenology. *Qualitative Health Research*, *29*(6), 900 – 907. https://doi.org/10.1177/10497323188175

Zahavi, D., & Martiny, K. M. (2019). Phenomenology in nursing studies: New perspectives. *International Journal of Nursing Studies*, *93*, 155 – 162. https://doi.org/10.1016/j.ijnurstu.2019.01.014

Zelizer, B. (2004). When facts, truth and reality are God-terms: On journalism's uneasy place in cultural studies. *Communication and Critical/Cultural Studies*, *1*(1), 100 – 119. https://doi.org/10.1080/1479142042000180953

Zelizer, B., Boczkowski, P. J., & Anderson, C. W. (2022). *The journalism manifesto.* Cambridge: Polity Press.

Index

Note: Page numbers in *italics* indicate figures, and references following "n" refer notes.

www.ingramcontent.com/pod-product-compliance
Lightning Source LLC
Chambersburg PA
CBHW030334270326
41926CB00010B/1624